SO YOU THINK YOU'RE A DALLAS COWBOYS FAN?

STARS, STATS, RECORDS, AND MEMORIES FOR TRUE DIEHARDS

JAIME ARON

SPORTS
PUBLISHING

Sports Publishing books may be purchased in bulk at special discounts for sales promotion, corporate gifts, fund-raising, or educational purposes. Special editions can also be created to specifications. For details, contact the Special Sales Department, Sports Publishing, 307 West 36th Street, 11th Floor, New York, NY 10018 or sportspubbooks@skyhorsepublishing.com.

Sports Publishing® is a registered trademark of Skyhorse Publishing, Inc.®, a Delaware corporation.

Visit our website at www.sportspubbooks.com.

10 9 8 7 6 5 4 3

Library of Congress Cataloging-in-Publication Data

Names: Aron, Jaime, author.
Title: So you think you're a Dallas Cowboys fan? : stars, stats, records, and
  memories for true diehards / Jaime Aron.
Description: New York : Sports Publishing, [2016]
Identifiers: LCCN 2016024071| ISBN 9781613219676 (alk. paper) | ISBN
  9781613219683 (Ebook)
Subjects: LCSH: Dallas Cowboys (Football team)--History. | Dallas Cowboys
  (Football team)--Miscellanea.
Classification: LCC GV956.D3 A766 2016 | DDC 796.332/64097642812--dc23 LC
record available at https://lccn.loc.gov/2016024071

Cover design by Tom Lau
Cover photo credit AP Photos

ISBN: 978-1-61321-967-6
Ebook ISBN: 978-1-61321-968-3

Printed in the United States of America

For Lori. Thanks for calling. TFA.

Contents

Contents

Introduction

Jerry Jones once told me he considers the Dallas Cowboys the most valuable property in the entertainment world. That's right—not just sports, *all of entertainment.*

His reasoning went something along these lines: The Cowboys are the most-watched team in the NFL. The NFL is the most-watched entity on television. Television is the dominant medium. Ergo, the Cowboys are kings.

While the pieces may not fit that easily, I believe there's a lot of truth to his logic. But here's the twist: my support of Jerry's premise is rooted not in his team's success, but in its failure.

As you surely know, the Cowboys entered the 2016 season having won a measly two playoff games in the past 20 seasons. Yet they've remained must-see TV. Merchandise continues to fly off the shelves, and sponsors flock to them. Jones parlayed it all into a palatial stadium, selling about 90,000 tickets per game.

That cements their status as "America's Team." Somewhere in there also exists whatever lured you to become a devoted follower. And no matter your level of knowledge, *So You Think You're a Dallas Cowboys Fan?* is aimed at you.

This is no typical questions-and-answers trivia book. Each question comes with an explanation—the story behind the answer. Such insights and anecdotes propel this book into a game-like stroll through team history. From great players to great plays, memorable games to historic seasons, they're all in here. Warning: some things you may want to forget are in here, too.

Like a football game, this book is broken into four quarters:

- Rookie Level is for newcomers and fans starting to build their knowledge base.
- Starter Level is where things start getting a little tougher.
- All-Pro Level is for those who know their stuff.
- Ring of Honor Level indicates special mastery.

As the questions get harder, the answers tend to get more detailed. So even if you're not at, say, the All-Pro level, you'll want to keep reading so you can keep learning.

Because team lore mostly revolves around the glory days, plenty of questions are devoted to those eras. Fear not, fans of more recent Cowboys teams. We'll also delve into the days of Tony Romo and Jason Witten, DeMarcus Ware and Dez Bryant.

In keeping with the notion of this being a guided tour of Cowboys lore, let me introduce myself, your tour guide.

Although I grew up in Houston during the "Luv Ya Blue" days, I always rooted for the Cowboys. I don't recall whether I was just being a contrarian or, like so many others, the magnetism of America's Team lured me in.

I attended my first game at Texas Stadium in October 1989, a few weeks after the Herschel Walker trade. I moved to Dallas in 1992, and the first game I covered for The Associated Press was the NFC Championship game following the '93 season. About six weeks later, I covered the news conference when Jerry Jones and Jimmy Johnson went their separate ways.

I became a regular on the AP's game-day coverage team the following season, when Barry Switzer was the coach. I moved up to being the AP's beat writer in 1999 (the end of the Chan Gailey era) and remained on the post through 2011 (the start of the Jason Garrett era). Along the way, I wrote three books about the club's gilded past, including *Dallas Cowboys: The Complete Illustrated History.*

Since leaving daily journalism, I've continued following the team. My Cowboys-loving wife wouldn't have it any other way.

OK, warmups are done. Time for kickoff.

ROOKIE LEVEL

We're going to start with a lot of fundamentals. The areas of emphasis in this section are the franchise's formative days and the greatest of the greats. Realizing that recent history fits in neither category, we'll cram some in anyway just to keep things current.

1 Who was the first player drafted by the Cowboys? *Answer on page 9.*

2 Nicknamed "Captain America," this player was so beloved that when he retired in 1980, NFL Films created its first-ever show honoring a single player. *Answer on page 10.*

3 Match game—pair the career statistic on the left with the Cowboy on the right. *Answer on page 11.*

QB with the most wins	Jason Witten
Most passing yards	Mel Renfro
Most rushing yards	Darren Woodson
Most receiving yards	DeMarcus Ware
Most catches	Tony Romo
Most tackles	Emmitt Smith
Most interceptions	Michael Irvin
Most sacks	Troy Aikman

4 When Tony Romo became the starting quarterback, whom did he replace? *Answer on page 12.*

5 The most frustrating year in Cowboys history has to be 1967. On the very first and the very last day of the calendar

year, they lost championship games that would have put them in Super Bowls I and II. They lost both games to the same team. Name that team. *Answer on page 13.*

6 The game on December 31, 1967, technically was known as the 1967 NFL Championship Game. However, it's often called by a nickname stemming from the frigid conditions: minus-5 degrees at kickoff with a wind chill of about minus-40. What is that memorable moniker? *Answer on page 14.*

7 Who am I? *Answer on page 16.*
   • My dazzling skills and flamboyant personality led to my perfectly fitting nickname.
   • How dazzling was I? I returned a kickoff 97 yards for a touchdown as a rookie—even though I played linebacker.
   • How flamboyant was I? I told the world that Steelers quarterback Terry Bradshaw couldn't spell "cat" if you spotted him the "c" and the "a."
   • After washing out of the NFL and enduring a long battle with drugs and alcohol, I won millions in the Texas Lottery.

8 As the Cowboys became a powerhouse in the 1960s, their defense picked up a nickname that was revived in the 1970s. What is it? *Answer on page 17.*

9 What was the nickname bestowed upon Troy Aikman, Emmitt Smith, and Michael Irvin? Give yourself a bonus if you know who came up with it. *Answer on page 18.*

10 Which team has the Cowboys beaten the most times in the Super Bowl? *Answer on page 19.*

11 Which team has the Cowboys faced the most times in the Super Bowl? *Answer on page 20.*

12 How many Super Bowls have the Cowboys played in? *Answer on page 21.*

13 Who was the founder/original owner of the Cowboys? *Answer on page 21.*

14 Part of the lore surrounding the team's entry into the NFL is that the founding owner bought the rights to a rival team's theme song. He swapped the song rights to the rival team's owner in exchange for the support needed to create the Cowboys. Name the rival team and give yourself a bonus if you can name the song. *Answer on page 23.*

15 The first president and general manager of the Cowboys held those jobs from before the NFL gave Dallas a franchise until two months after Jerry Jones bought the team. Name him. *Answer on page 25.*

16 There's only one statue outside AT&T Stadium. Who was so respected and revered that he received this larger-than-life tribute? *Answer on page 26.*

17 Who am I? *Answer on page 27.*

- I became the starting quarterback after Roger Staubach retired.

- While waiting my turn as the backup, I was the team's punter—a job I kept while starting at quarterback.

- I led the team to three straight NFC title games, but no Super Bowls.

18 On January 3, 1983, _____ became the first player ever to run 99 yards for a touchdown, setting a record that can be tied but never broken. *Answer on page 28.*

19 Among Tom Landry's most incredible accomplishments is an NFL-record streak of _____ consecutive winning seasons. (Fill in the blank.) *Answer on page 30.*

20 Tom Landry obviously coached—and won—the most games in Cowboys history. Who is No. 2 on those lists? *Answer on page 31.*

21 From the franchise's formative years to the Jerry Jones era, the team's draft guru was a self-made scout, a guy who created an unusual baby photography business that ran itself, giving him the time and money needed for his hobby of studying football players. Name him. *Answer on page 34.*

22 This "Dandy" fellow was the team's first breakout personality. Teammates loved his toughness, and women swooned over his looks and charm. Fans were split, with many critical of his play. Upon retiring, he enjoyed a successful second career in the *Monday Night Football* broadcasting booth. *Answer on page 35.*

23 Name all the stadiums the Cowboys have called home. (Bonus: name the year the team debuted in each building.) *Answer on page 37.*

24 The hole in the roof of Texas Stadium developed a celestial myth around its origin. What was that heavenly saying? (Bonus if you know who came up with it.) *Answer on page 39.*

25 Roger Staubach coined the term "Hail Mary" after completing a 50-yard pass to _____, his go-to guy on many big plays throughout their years together. *Answer on page 39.*

26 Only once in Super Bowl history has the MVP award been shared by two players. It happened, of course, to the Cowboys. Which two players were honored as co-MVPs? (Bonus points if you know which Super Bowl.) *Answer on page 41.*

27 Who am I? *Answer on page 42.*
- During a blowout victory in the Super Bowl following the 1992 season, I almost returned a fumble for a touchdown. But I started celebrating too soon, and Buffalo's Don Beebe jarred the ball loose.
- On Thanksgiving the following season, I touched a blocked kick, bringing back to life what would've been a dead ball and allowing the Miami Dolphins to win a memorable, snowy game.
- In recent years, I've been an assistant defensive line coach for the Cowboys.

28 Just as Jason Witten was considered Tony Romo's security blanket at tight end, _____ filled that role for Troy Aikman. *Answer on page 44.*

29 Only once in Super Bowl history has a member of the losing team been named the game's MVP. Who earned this unusual accolade? (Hint: he's in the Ring of Honor.) *Answer on page 45.*

30 Name the dynamic duo that locked down the safety position for the Cowboys in the 1970s. *Answer on page 46.*

31 The Cowboys jump-started their rebuilding in the middle of the 1989 season when they traded Herschel Walker to the _____. *Answer on page 47.*

32 When Terrell Owens was playing for the San Francisco 49ers and celebrated a touchdown by visiting the Cowboys' logo at midfield of Texas Stadium not just once but twice, which defensive back defended the star with a flying takedown of T.O. the second time? *Answer on page 49.*

33 Probably the most agonizing dropped pass in Cowboys history came in the Super Bowl following the 1978 season, against the Pittsburgh Steelers, when Roger Staubach hit future Hall of Famer _____ right between the numbers in the end zone. *Answer on page 50.*

34 This undrafted safety was such a standout on punts and kickoffs that the NFL created a special-teams position on the Pro Bowl roster. He went on to play the second-most games in team history. Who is he? *Answer on page 52.*

35 On the rare occasions when this fullback caught a pass or took a handoff, fans roared "Moooooose!" What's his real name? *Answer on page 52.*

36 It's been quite a while since the Cowboys won a Super Bowl. Who was named the game's MVP way back then? *Answer on page 53.*

37 Who am I? *Answer on page 54.*
- I won two gold medals and set two world records at the 1964 Olympics, earning me the title "World's Fastest Human."
- Zone defenses became common in the NFL to counter my blazing speed.
- I still hold the club's career record for receiving touchdowns.

38 The Cowboys have had plenty of great offensive linemen, but only one guy was so versatile that he made All-Pro at guard and tackle, so dominant that he made the NFL's All-Decade Team for the 1990s and 2000s, and so strong that he bench-pressed 700 pounds. Name this ferocious force. *Answer on page 55.*

39 Going into the 2016 season, only one kicker in NFL history has made 90 percent of his field goal attempts, and he did so for the Cowboys. Who is he? *Answer on page 57.*

40 Long before the current cartoon-faced character Rowdy, the Cowboys had an unofficial mascot in _____, a fan who wore chaps and a vest featuring the Cowboys' star logo and carried a toy gun. *Answer on page 58.*

ROOKIE LEVEL – ANSWERS

1 Bob Lilly turned out to be not only the first draft pick in Cowboys history, but also the club's first star player, first member of the Ring of Honor, and first representative in the Pro Football Hall of Fame. For all these reasons, he'll forever be known as "Mr. Cowboy."

Lilly was a defensive tackle with size, strength, and speed. Offensive linemen might have been able to match him in one or two areas, but rarely in all three. He made the NFL's All-Decade Team for the 1960s and 1970s.

Bob Lilly savors a victory cigar after the Cowboys won Super Bowl VI, the only championship in the career of "Mr. Cowboy." (AP Photo)

The interesting twist to Lilly's being the first pick is that he was part of the 1961 draft, and the Cowboys began playing in 1960.

In an attempt to beat the upstart AFL from snagging star college players, the NFL draft for the 1960 season was held on November 30, 1959. The Cowboys weren't officially added to the league until January 1960, so, simply put, they missed it. Their original team was stocked with mostly has-beens and never-weres plucked from other teams through an expansion draft. That collection of players went 0-11-1 in the first season.

Dallas had traded away what would've been the No. 2 overall pick in the 1961 draft, so its first choice was No. 13.

Lilly never missed a game over his 14 seasons. Seeing as the Cowboys didn't win a single game before he arrived, that means he was part of every victory in team history until he retired following the 1974 season.

2 Roger Staubach first won over football fans in 1963, as a junior at Navy, when his wild scrambles and accurate passes propelled him to the Heisman Trophy and led the Midshipmen to a No. 2 ranking.

His pro career was delayed by his military commitment. He served his country from 1965 to 1969, even spending time in Vietnam. Yet he never gave up his dream of playing pro football. While in the Navy, he saved up his leave time to attend Cowboys' training camp. Coincidentally, the same day Staubach left the military for good, Don Meredith retired.

While Staubach actually started—and won—the first game of his rookie season (1969), he only got the chance because Craig Morton was injured. Morton returned to lead the Cowboys that year and the next. Staubach finally became the full-time starter in mid-1971. Dallas won the rest of its games that season, including its first-ever Super Bowl title. Staubach was the MVP of that game.

Staubach was the main quarterback for nine seasons. The Cowboys played in four Super Bowls during that time, winning two and losing the others by four points each.

When all was said and done, Staubach retired as the top-rated quarterback in NFL history. He's also remembered for his comebacks: 23 game-winning drives, including 15 fourth-quarter comebacks.

3 While **Tony Romo** lacks the Super Bowl rings of Troy Aikman and Roger Staubach, he has them beat in many statistical areas, including **passing yards**. He went into the 2016 season with 34,154 yards. A good chunk of that has come from throwing to his good buddy **Jason Witten**, who owns the team record for **most catches** (1,020).

Aikman remains the leader in **victories** with 94. That doesn't include another 11 in the postseason—three of them in Super Bowls. A big part of his success was playing with two guys who would later join him in the Hall of Fame, Emmitt Smith and Michael Irvin.

Smith is not only the team's career **rushing** leader (17,162 yards), but also the NFL's rushing king. (His career total is 18,355 yards, padded by two seasons in Arizona.) **Irvin**'s 11,904 yards **receiving** are the most in team history, although Witten could pass him in 2016.

Mel Renfro split his career between safety and cornerback, yet no matter where he lined up, he found the football. His 52 **interceptions** are easily the most in team history; the next highest has 44 (Everson Walls).

Of all the great pass-catchers in team history, Jason Witten has the most receptions. He could pass Michael Irvin for the most receiving yards during the 2016 season. (AP Photo/Elaine Thompson)

Darren Woodson was a college linebacker turned safety in the NFL. His 813 **tackles** are tops in club history. While a small percentage came on special teams, the fact that a player of his stature always wanted to be out there on punts and kickoffs showed what a gamer he was.

DeMarcus Ware is the **sack** leader, with 117. Sacks didn't become an official statistic until 1982, but his total still tops the club's unofficial tally of 114 racked up by Harvey Martin.

4 Drew Bledsoe fired toward the end zone for Terry Glenn late in the second quarter of the sixth game of the 2006 season. A member of the New York Giants caught it instead. And just like that, Bledsoe's NFL career would prove to be over.

Romo replaced him for the second half, and, well, you know the rest.

Bledsoe arrived in 2005 and served as a solid "bus driver" for coach Bill Parcells, leading Dallas to a winning record (9-7). But in the summer of '06, Parcells let it be known that the undrafted Romo was coming on strong.

Bledsoe, of course, had seen it all before. In New England, he lost his starting job to a then-unproven backup named Tom Brady.

Romo was the 2002 Division I-AA player of the year for Eastern Illinois University but went undrafted. The Denver Broncos offered more money than Dallas did, but Romo looked at the Cowboys' roster and figured he had a better chance of working his way up. Perhaps that was the first clue of how good he was at reading the opposition.

5 From 1960 to 1964, the Cowboys made a slow climb to respectability, never winning more than five games in a 14-game season. They improved to 7-7 in '65, and then, finally, things clicked. They became a team to be reckoned with in '66, going 10-3-1 and winning their division.

The playoff structure back then was pretty basic. There were two divisions, and the champions of each met to decide the league's champion. The Cowboys happened to hit their stride at the right time: 1966 was the first time the NFL and AFL agreed to have their champions square off in another game. (Quick historic aside: Modern-day marketing types would cringe at the boring title "AFL-NFL Championship Game." The next two years it went by "World Championship Game." The moniker "Super Bowl" was finally attached for the fourth installment, in January 1971. Roman numerals arrived the following year, which happens to be when the Cowboys arrived at the big game.)

On January 1, 1967, the Cowboys didn't just play in their first-ever postseason game, they played it at home with a trip to the first-ever Super Bowl on the line. (This was such a big deal that the Cotton Bowl game was moved up a day, to December 31, 1966. It was the first time ever that that game was held in December; the second wasn't until 2015, when it was bumped up to accommodate college football's new playoff format.)

In that New Year's Day game, the Cowboys faced the reigning NFL champs from Green Bay. The Packers weren't only more experienced in games of such magnitude; they also had a better season—12-2, compared to the Cowboys' 10-3-1. (The game was played in Dallas, because it had been decided long before that the winner of that division would be the home team. Teams weren't seeded in the postseason until 1975.)

The Cowboys erased an early 14-point deficit to tie the game at 14, only to fall behind again by 14 points. Then came another rally. An infamous false start penalty on lineman Jim Boeke hurt the potential tying drive in the closing minutes. On the same play, Dan Reeves got poked in the eye, leaving him with double vision. That became a problem on the next play, when Reeves tried catching a pass in the end zone and reached for the mirage instead of the ball. The drive fizzled, and instead of going to Super Bowl I, Dallas lost, 34-27.

On December 31, 1967, the teams met again, only this time in Green Bay. More on that game in the next answer.

6 Known as the "Ice Bowl," this game remains unforgettable in many ways to the Cowboys who played in it.

The bad memories go beyond losing—and, as with the previous season's NFL Championship game, losing in agonizing fashion. It's about the lifelong aches and pains stemming from playing in those brutal conditions.

Let's first set the stage on how this rematch came to be.

The NFL had broken into four divisions in 1967. Dallas, Cleveland, the Los Angeles Rams, and Green Bay were the winners, so the former two and the latter two squared off in division-round games. The Cowboys crushed the Browns, 52-14, for their first postseason victory, and the Packers dispatched the Rams.

When the Cowboys arrived in Wisconsin, the temperature was in the teens. An $80,000 underground heating system was supposed to keep the field playable. Then a blast of cold air from Canada rolled through, sinking temperatures well below zero.

A college marching band refused to perform, fearing their lips would get stuck to their instruments. Officials faced the same problem with their whistles. One guy ripped his lips on the first blow; everyone wised up after that, keeping Vaseline on their mouthpieces.

Remember, this was back in the macho days when people who drank water were considered weak. Coaches on both sidelines urged players to show their toughness by not wearing gloves or other protection.

Just like the New Year's Day game, the Packers jumped ahead, 14-0. But Dallas rallied to lead, 17-14, in the third quarter.

With 16 seconds left, Green Bay was about two feet shy of the goal line. The Packers knew they had one play left. Considering the conditions, even a short field goal was no sure thing. And that would only mean they'd have to keep playing.

On a quarterback sneak, Bart Starr got into the end zone by following a block by right guard Jerry Kramer. While Dallas

Tenacious defenders like Randy White continued the tradition of Dallas's "Doomsday Defense." White was nicknamed "Manster" because he was half-man, half-monster. (AP Photo/Ron Heflin)

particular reason except it sounded sexier than Flex defense— and the name caught on."

9 Although Troy Aikman, Emmitt Smith, and Michael Irvin had been teammates for several years before Barry Switzer arrived, he's the one who tabbed them as "The Triplets."

The name stuck at least partly because of how much the trio embraced it. While each was a star in his own right, each also knew the team's success came from how great they were as a group. Having a single term that referred to them collectively just made sense.

"I always loved it when they called us that," Aikman said through tears at his retirement news conference.

They arrived in consecutive years—first Irvin (1988), then Aikman ('89), then Smith ('90). They departed in that same order, with Irvin retiring after the 1999 season, Aikman getting released and then retiring after the 2000 season, and Smith getting cut after the 2002 season, then retiring after two seasons in Arizona.

Officially, the Triplet Era was 1990-99. Dallas went 101-59 in that span, winning three Super Bowls in four years and making the playoffs in eight of those 10 seasons.

"You could take one of us lightly if you want to," Smith said, "but the other two are going to hurt you pretty bad."

The Aikman-Smith-Irvin trio led the club in passing, rushing, and receiving every year from 1991 to 1998. To put that eight-year run in perspective, the next-longest streak for any trio in franchise history is four in a row.

It was only fitting that they went into the Ring of Honor together during a *Monday Night Football* game in 2005. They're also reunited in the Hall of Fame, although that order of induction went Aikman (2006), Irvin (2007), and Smith (2010).

10 The Buffalo Bills had the misfortune of having the greatest era in franchise history at the same time as the Cowboys.

Buffalo went to an amazing four straight Super Bowls following the 1990-93 seasons. The Bills only came close to winning the first, losing to Bill Parcells and the New York Giants when Scott Norwood missed a 47-yard field goal in the final seconds.

That experience made them hungry to get back—and keep going back. Yet it also seemed to scar them.

They'd lost two straight Super Bowls when they squared off in the big game against the upstart Cowboys in January 1993.

Dallas's inexperience proved blissful on the way to a lopsided victory. In a rematch the following January, the Bills actually led, 13-6, at halftime. Troy Aikman was headed into the locker room feeling pretty lousy until he looked across the field and saw the body language of guys like quarterback Jim Kelly, running back Thurman Thomas, receiver Andre Reed, and defensive tackle Bruce Smith.

"You would have thought they were a team that just felt that something bad was going to happen, that they were snakebit in Super Bowls," Aikman said.

Perhaps they were. Buffalo got shut out in the second half on the way to a 30-13 Dallas victory, leaving the Bills 0-2 in Super Bowls against the Cowboys.

11 The Pittsburgh Steelers own this distinction, as well as the distinction of being the only team with multiple Super Bowl victories over the Cowboys.

Just like Buffalo had the misfortune of facing great Dallas teams, the Cowboys of the 1970s had the misfortune of facing the Steelers during their "Steel Curtain" heyday, when they had a squad that's considered among the greatest in NFL history.

Dallas hung tough in both Super Bowl losses to Pittsburgh, dropping each by only four points.

Twenty years after that first defeat, the Triplets-era Cowboys helped the franchise secure a bit of revenge by beating the Steelers in a Super Bowl.

Cowboys fans who insist on always rooting against the Steelers because of those two Super Bowl losses will be happy to note that Pittsburgh came out on the wrong end of the Super Bowl following the 2010 season—the first, and still only, title game held at the Cowboys' home stadium.

12 The Cowboys have played in eight Super Bowls, winning five.

It's worth noting that their three losses are by a combined 11 points.

Here's a quick recap:

DATE	GAME	SCORE
Jan. 17, 1971	Super Bowl V	Baltimore Colts 16, Cowboys 13
Jan. 16, 1972	Super Bowl VI	Cowboys 24, Miami Dolphins 3
Jan. 18, 1976	Super Bowl X	Pittsburgh Steelers 21, Cowboys 17
Jan. 15, 1978	Super Bowl XII	Cowboys 27, Denver Broncos 10
Jan. 21, 1979	Super Bowl XIII	Pittsburgh Steelers 35, Cowboys 31
Jan. 31, 1993	Super Bowl XXVII	Cowboys 52, Buffalo Bills 17
Jan. 30, 1994	Super Bowl XXVIII	Cowboys 30, Buffalo Bills 13
Jan. 28, 1996	Super Bowl XXX	Cowboys 27, Pittsburgh Steelers 17

While the Cowboys were the first team to reach eight Super Bowls, the Steelers, Patriots, and Broncos have all caught up and share that record.

Dallas's five Super Bowl wins are tied with San Francisco for second-most. The 49ers won their fifth the year before the Cowboys won their fifth. The Steelers have since caught and passed them with six titles.

13 Clint Murchison Jr. loved the first NFL team in town, the 1952 Dallas Texans.

Never heard of 'em? There's a good reason. Back then, the locals believed that football was played by high schoolers on Friday nights and by Southwest Conference teams on Saturday; Sunday was reserved for church and family. Pro football never had a chance. It was such a bad fit that the team played just four home games before owners gave up, playing out the season on the road.

The '52 Texans left two legacies, though. They're the answer to another trivia question (last NFL team to fold), and they became the inspiration for Murchison to bring the NFL back to Dallas.

Murchison was a short, stocky guy who wore glasses and a buzz cut. He was also part of an oil-rich family worth more than $1 billion (the equivalent of more than $11 billion in today's dollars). After years of trying to buy a team and move it to Dallas, he switched gears and went for an expansion team.

His efforts got a boost from—of all things—the start of the rival AFL.

One of the driving forces in that league was the son of another oil tycoon, Lamar Hunt, who was determined to bring a team to Dallas. The NFL—fearing it would lose a chance to plant its flag in fertile soil—suddenly became more interested in Murchison's quest.

On January 28, 1960, his dream turned into a reality. He is also the person who chose "Cowboys" as the name and blue as the primary color.

It's a shame Murchison is not in the Ring of Honor, if for no reason but to prompt fans into asking, "Who's that?" Because, in addition to his patriarchal role in team history, he was a fascinating character.

His personality is reminiscent of Jerry Jones's in that he was a fun-loving carouser who was willing to spend big bucks to get what he wanted. For instance, he owned a Caribbean island and an exclusive hotel in California. The MIT graduate also had a quick wit: before the Cowboys' first Super Bowl, he sent Tom Landry the following note: "I have taught you all I can. From now on, you're on your own."

That leads to the key difference between Murchison and Jones. The founder was strictly hands-off, letting his football experts make all the football decisions. (Another line from Murchison: "I do not offer suggestions to Landry. Furthermore, Landry never makes suggestions as to how I conduct my sixth-grade football team—which, incidentally, is undefeated. We have a professional standoff.")

Drugs, drinking, gambling, and womanizing caught up to Murchison in the 1980s. He sold the team in 1984 to try to pay off his debts. Murchison died three years later. He was 63 and owed creditors hundreds of millions of dollars.

14 George Preston Marshall, owner of the Washington Redskins, was the biggest obstacle to Clint Murchison's bid for an expansion team.

In 1958, Marshall considered selling his team to Murchison. The more they negotiated, the more they disliked each other. Still, they got to the verge of striking a deal, when Marshall tried changing the terms. That did it: Murchison walked away.

In addition to holding a grudge against Murchison, Marshall had the southernmost team in the NFL and wanted to keep it that way. While Washington may not seem like a Southern city, it identified that way enough that when the team's fight song—"Hail to the Redskins"—was written, it included the line "Fight for old Dixie." (It has since been changed to "old D.C.")

The song's lyrics were penned by Marshall's wife, a former silent-movie actress. But the song's rights were held by Barnee Breeskin, a D.C.-area band leader who'd composed the song.

Around the time that Murchison sought Marshall's support, Breeskin had a falling out with Marshall. Recognizing that the enemy of my enemy is my friend, Breeskin sold the song to Murchison.

That left Marshall with a choice: let Dallas into the league and have his beloved song continue to play at home games or keep Dallas out and ask his wife to write a new fight song.

Obviously, you know what he chose.

The stodgy Marshall remained a fun target for the prankster Murchison.

At halftime of the 1961 game in Washington, Santa Claus was to be pulled across the field by a pack of Alaskan huskies. Murchison's elaborate plan to disrupt the show included flying in crates full of chickens from Texas and having spies spread chicken feed across the field the night before the game. As "Jingle Bells" played, the chickens would be released. The birds would go for the feed and the dogs would go after the birds.

Alas, a stadium worker heard some clucking and prevented the grand plan from being enacted. But that's not the end of the story.

After complaining to NFL commissioner Pete Rozelle, Marshall received phone calls in which he heard no words—only clucking sounds. He changed his phone number several times, and for a while the prank calls continued to find him.

Then, before the 1962 game in Washington, as the band played "Hail to the Redskins," four banners were unfurled, at each side of the 50-yard line and behind each end zone. Each bore a single word: CHICKENS. Two men dressed in chicken suits charged toward the field, handing out colored eggs along the way. One of these chicken men was stopped, but the other made it onto the field. As the national anthem blared, he pulled out a live chicken and released it. He then jiggled around, avoiding guards who were chasing him, spun a cartwheel, and hightailed it out of there.

After Lombardi left for Green Bay, Landry was in line to become the next coach of the Giants. The Houston Oilers tried getting him to be their first coach. But on December 28, 1959—that's right, a month before the Cowboys were voted into existence—Schramm hired Landry. (In fact, Landry was introduced as the head coach of the Dallas Rangers, as they'd yet to settle on a permanent nickname.)

The Cowboys struggled in their early years, but owner Clint Murchison Jr. believed so strongly in Landry that he gave him a 10-year contract extension. It was a brilliant move. But by the 1980s, support for Landry was waning. Truth be told, fans were more than ready for a change. Once it happened, the problem was the way Jerry Jones cut ties—by flying to Landry's vacation home near Austin and replacing him with an unproven college coach. Who was this brash new owner? The outpouring of emotion over Landry's ousting showed what an icon he'd become.

Landry's career record is 250-162-6. The wins are third most in NFL history, behind only Don Shula and George Halas. His postseason mark of 20-16 included a league record for wins until it was recently topped by Bill Belichick.

17 Danny White is among the most star-crossed figures in franchise history.

He completed more passes, threw for more touchdowns, and had a higher completion percentage than Roger Staubach. He started more playoff games than Troy Aikman. He had a higher winning percentage than Tony Romo.

He also failed to reach a Super Bowl despite reaching the NFC Championship game in each of his first three seasons at the helm. In the second of those—the game known for

"The Catch"—Dwight Clark's go-ahead touchdown grab could've been overcome with a field goal on Dallas's final drive. But after reaching midfield, White was hit from behind and fumbled.

Until Romo wins a Super Bowl, he and White will be lumped together, a pair of regular-season successes who put up great stats but never won—much less, got to—the big one. The agony of White's tenure is perhaps best summed up by a flub in a *Monday Night Football* game in 1983. On a fourth down, White talked Tom Landry out of punting, but only so he could try drawing the Redskins offsides. He was supposed to call a timeout if that didn't work. But White saw a defense that was overloaded in the middle, so he called for an outside run. The Redskins snuffed it out, and cameras caught Landry screaming, "No! No! No, Danny, no!"

Of course, there's something else we need to discuss about White's legacy—his punting. He still holds the club record for attempts, with an average distance of 40.2 that remains among the best. He retired with the highest net average for a career, most punts inside the 20, and the longest streak without getting a punt blocked.

18 The final game of the strike-shortened 1982 season was on a Monday night in Minnesota. Win or lose, it had no bearing on the Cowboys' playoff seeding.

By the fourth quarter, they sure looked like a team playing a meaningless game.

Danny White threw an interception that was returned for a touchdown, putting the Vikings ahead, 24-13. Kickoff returner Timmy Newsome muffed the ensuing kick, so Dallas started on its 1-yard line.

And get this: fullback Ron Springs thought the Cowboys were going to run a play that didn't involve him. So he stayed on the sideline, leaving Dallas with just 10 men on the field.

That gave Springs a good view of what happened next.

Even without the benefit of a lead blocker, Tony Dorsett ran right through the middle of the offensive line, cut toward the right sideline, and zoomed into NFL history with a 99-yard touchdown. It was the longest run from scrimmage the league had ever seen—or could ever see. The previous best was 97 yards, accomplished by Andy Uram of the Packers in 1939 and Bob Gage of the Steelers in 1949.

"I was in awe of the play myself," said Minnesota coach Bud Grant, whose shame over allowing such a run was eased by having won the game. "He saw a crack and exploited it."

Vision, speed, and the quickness to make defenders miss turned Tony Dorsett into one of the greatest running backs in NFL history. (AP Photo)

Dorsett's shoes from that play are in the Hall of Fame. There's a bust of Dorsett there, too.

Dorsett ran for 12,739 yards in his career, the second-most in league history—trailing only Walter Payton—at the time he retired. Dorsett is now eighth on the career list.

Acquired in one of Tex Schramm's classic draft swindles, Dorsett was brought along slowly as a rookie yet still cracked the 1,000-yard mark. He became the first player to do so the first five seasons of his career, a streak interrupted only because of the strike in 1982. He returned to the 1,000-yard plateau the next three seasons.

Because Dorsett was relatively slim at 5-foot-11, 192 pounds, Tom Landry was always cautious about how much of a pounding his star running back took. Landry figured 20 carries a game was enough. Dorsett averaged 17.5 carries per game over his 11 seasons.

This leads to a great, unanswerable debate: Would Dorsett have run for even more yards with more carries? Or would more of a workload have worn him out sooner?

Considering that Dorsett missed only three games during his first nine seasons doing it Landry's way, it's fair to say things worked out just fine. Still, it's always fun to wonder about what might've been.

19 From 1966 to 1985—an amazing 20-year stretch—the Cowboys had a winning record. To appreciate this fully, you need to view it from a wider context.

Let's take the last 100 years in all four major U.S. pro sports.

In baseball, only the New York Yankees have topped 20 straight winning seasons, doing it twice. They set the unlikely-to-be-broken record of 39 straight from 1926 to 1964 and went into 2016 in the midst of a 23-year run.

In hockey, three teams have topped 20 straight winning seasons. The Montreal Canadiens went 32 in a row, the Boston Bruins reached 29, and the Detroit Red Wings are in the midst of a 24-year run.

In basketball, it's never happened—at least not yet. The San Antonio Spurs are at 19, matching the record set by the Utah Jazz.

In football, the next-best mark is 16, set by the San Francisco 49ers and their Bay Area counterparts, the Oakland Raiders. (Oakland's streak began with five winning seasons in the AFL.)

The New England Patriots are at 15 in a row. That means they are only 75 percent of the way there.

There's also this: in the 30 seasons since Landry's streak ended, the Cowboys have a *total* of 14 winning seasons. The longest streak? A measly six in a row.

20 You may be surprised to know that it's the current coach, Jason Garrett.

In 5.5 seasons, Garrett has climbed past every one of Tom Landry's successors . . . that is, in the basic categories of regular-season games coached and won.

Garrett went into the 2016 season with a career record of 45-43. Throw in his 1-1 postseason record, and that's a total of 90 games.

Garrett topped his former coach, Jimmy Johnson, who went 44-36 in the regular season and 7-1 in the postseason.

Johnson, of course, inherited a talent-starved team and then further stripped down the roster, bottoming out at

1-15 before putting together all the right pieces to win two Super Bowls. He left Dallas on a six-game postseason winning streak. Impact-wise, Johnson is easily No. 2 to Landry. (Another of Garrett's former coaches in Dallas, Barry Switzer, guided the Cowboys to a Super Bowl title. Even if Switzer rode to it with the roster inherited from Johnson, you can easily argue that puts him ahead of Garrett in terms of true production. We'll cover the Switzer era in a later section.)

Let's get back to Garrett and give him his due.

His story actually begins with his dad, Jim Garrett, who joined the club as a scout for Tom Landry and Tex Schramm in the early 1980s. He remained with the organization after Jerry Jones bought the club and lasted all the way until 2004, making him among the longest holdovers between those eras.

Jason was a teenager when Jim was hired by Dallas. Jason went on to play quarterback at Princeton, where he was named the Ivy League Player of the Year in 1988. He bounced around for several years, going from the Saints' developmental squad to spending a year as an assistant coach at Princeton, then playing in the World League and the Canadian Football League. He landed on the Dallas practice squad in 1992 and made the club the following year as a twenty-seven-year-old rookie.

His most famous game came on Thanksgiving Day in 1994 against Brett Favre, Reggie White, and the Packers. It was just the second start of his career; he'd been pulled early from the first one. Considering how slowly he started against the Packers, Garrett might've been pulled again, but Switzer had no other legitimate option. Garrett rebounded to guide Dallas to five touchdowns in a span of 18:40. The Cowboys scored 36 points in the second half, a club record, on their way to a memorable 42-31 victory.

Garrett remained with the Cowboys through 1999, then played for the New York Giants and Tampa Bay Buccaneers. "Played" is too strong of a term, as his last snap came in 2000, yet he remained on their rosters through 2004. He lingered not for his arm but for his mind. He was already viewed as an up-and-coming coach, someone who'd played for—and learned from—Johnson, Norv Turner, Ernie Zampese, Sean Payton, and Jon Gruden.

His first official NFL coaching job was as quarterbacks coach for Nick Saban on the Dolphins in 2005. When Bill Parcells resigned as head coach of the Cowboys following the 2006 season, Jones interviewed Garrett and immediately decided to hire him . . . only he wasn't sure yet which job Garrett would have. It had to be a promotion to pry him from Miami. Jones decided to make Garrett the offensive coordinator and went with Wade Phillips—an experienced head coach whose strength was defense—for the top job.

Dallas enjoyed a great season in 2007, and Garrett became a hot commodity on the coaching market. Baltimore and Atlanta were interested in his leading their teams, but he made the extraordinary move of turning down both head-coaching opportunities. It was another indication that he'd eventually replace Phillips.

His promotion came midway through the 2010 season. Taking over a team that defied high expectations by starting 1-7, Garrett guided the Cowboys to a 5-3 mark the rest of the way, starting with a stirring road win against the Giants.

Mediocrity followed. Dallas went 8-8 the next three seasons. A breakthrough 12-4 campaign in 2014 was capped by a playoff win and an excruciating loss the next week in Green Bay; had officials given Dez Bryant credit for what looked like a catch at the 1-inch line, the Cowboys would've had a chance to win and advance to the NFC Championship game—and perhaps beyond. Controversy aside, everyone felt good about the team's direction going into 2015. Then Tony Romo got hurt and things fell apart, ending in a 4-12 flop.

A $30 million, five-year contract extension signed before the 2015 season helped Garrett keep the job. But that was only part of what cooled that potentially hot seat.

There's a strong bond between the Jones and Garrett families, one that has Jerry rooting for Jason to enjoy a Landry-like tenure. Garrett needs more 12-4s than 4-12s, but he's already proven that he can weather a storm of extended mediocrity.

21 Gil Brandt may be the first draft fan in NFL history or at least the first person enthralled enough to turn it into a hobby, then an obsession, then a career.

It all began when Brandt was a student at the University of Wisconsin. Pretending to be a high school coach, he called college teams and asked for game film. From those, he culled his list of top prospects.

He pulled off another shrewd scheme after college. By giving cameras to nurses in hospital nurseries, he was able to provide parents with photos of their bundles of joy. Remember, this was the 1950s, before cameras were common. Hospitals added a fee for the pictures to the parents' bills, and Brandt collected enough profit to fund his ongoing studies of football players.

One of his neighbors in Milwaukee was receiving great Elroy "Crazy Legs" Hirsch. While playing for the Los Angeles Rams, Hirsch told his bosses that if they needed any information about college players, they should call Brandt. That is how

Brandt became introduced to Tex Schramm, who was then the general manager of the Rams.

When it was time to stock the Cowboys' initial roster, they didn't have the benefit of a college draft. As you may recall, it had already been held when the team was voted into existence. So Schramm empowered Brandt to sign whomever he could. Schramm later said, "He sent me 30 contracts in two days and I had to tell him to slow down. I also had to hire him full-time as our personnel director."

Between Brandt's wily ways and an ahead-of-its-time computerized scouting system, the Cowboys' talent procurement department was the lifeblood of the organization for two decades.

Although Brandt was swept aside when Jerry Jones took over, he's remained a draft guru, offering his insights via NFL.com and frequent TV and radio appearances.

22 Don Meredith's career with the Cowboys plays out like a country-western song, the kind he often sang between plays.

Raised in the East Texas town of Mount Vernon, he starred in football and basketball in high school, then became a football star at SMU.

He happened to be coming out of college the same year the Cowboys were starting. However, it was also the same year the Dallas Texans of the AFL were starting.

As mentioned several times, the draft had already occurred without Dallas, and Meredith had been chosen by Chicago. Bears owner George Halas realized how important it would be for the Cowboys to have Meredith—and for the Texans *not* to have Meredith—so Halas swapped the quarterback's rights to Dallas for a small price: a third-round pick in 1962. By then, the Cowboys had already persuaded Meredith to stick with the established league by giving him a $150,000, five-year "personal services" contract; this ensured he'd cash in even if Dallas somehow didn't get, or keep, an NFL team.

Meredith made only one start his rookie year, but the Cowboys became his team starting in 1961. He took a pounding for several years—from defenses bolting through makeshift offensive lines, from Tom Landry, and from fans.

Landry was somewhat relentless in his criticism of Meredith, and fans followed his lead. Teammates, however, were incredibly loyal because they knew that beyond his freewheeling, fun-loving façade, Meredith pushed himself. As he once said, "It wasn't a matter of courage as much as determination. Nobody is going to beat me."

Don Meredith led the Cowboys from start-up to the brink of greatness with his scrambling, passing, and leadership. (AP Photo/File)

Yet the hard hits of every kind eventually broke him. After getting benched during the 1968 playoff loss to Cleveland, he retired a few months later. He was only thirty-one.

But he was far from done.

Meredith went through some rough years, then re-emerged as the colorful, folksy sidekick to Howard Cosell on *Monday Night Football*. You knew a game was out of reach when he warbled one of his country tunes, "The Party's Over." In his early days in the booth, he got in some good licks on Landry when he refused to pick between Craig Morton and Roger Staubach as his quarterback.

Meredith remained in the public eye as a broadcaster, actor, and popular pitchman for Lipton tea. Then he turned out the lights, becoming an intensely private man for the final decades of his life, rarely attending Cowboys events or anything else involving big crowds.

"I'm very thankful about where I'm from and who I am," he told the *Dallas Morning News* in 2009, in a rare interview that proved to be his last. Meredith died in 2010. He was seventy-two.

23 The Cowboys debuted in 1960 at the Cotton Bowl, sharing the venue with the Dallas Texans of the AFL. College football was king then, and there was a question of whether pro football would even take root. The NFL and AFL teams knew that even if pro football took off, only one of them would survive. Even though the Texans had more success, facing the established teams and bigger-named stars in the NFL helped the Cowboys claim the city—and stadium—for themselves.

Eventually, ownership and fans got tired of the rickety old place in Fair Park. So up went Texas Stadium in Irving. It was an audacious move in every way, including the use of bonds (the forerunner of Personal Seat Licenses) to help pay for it and the fact that it was in a sparsely populated suburb (outside its namesake hometown of Dallas). The facility was considered state-of-the-art, from its amenities to its giant hole in the roof. The Cowboys moved in midway through the 1971 season; they went on to win their first Super Bowl that postseason.

In 2009, the Cowboys traded up again, moving to yet another city, Arlington. Local taxpayers agreed to pay $325 million, with the team footing the bill for everything else. The tab eventually escalated well above $1.1 billion and set a new standard for stadiums everywhere in size, quality, and other

Texas Stadium was a state-of-the-art facility when it opened during the 1971 season. The Cowboys won their first championship that year, and four more while playing under the hole in the roof. (AP Photo/Mike Murphy)

mind-blowing touches like the enormous overhead scoreboard, field-level bars and suites, standing-room-only area in the end zones, and more.

24 Credit linebacker D.D. Lewis for uttering the epic line about Texas Stadium's roof being left open "so God can watch his favorite team play."

The real story?

Original owner Clint Murchison Jr. wanted to top the buzz surrounding the Astrodome in Houston. He also wanted something different. He came up with a design that he hoped could provide the best of both worlds—indoors and outdoors.

Having studied engineering and math at Duke and MIT, Murchison believed his partial roof would keep fans comfy while leaving players to endure whatever Mother Nature threw at them. Actually, that was the story he concocted while trying to save on utility bills. The way he had the roof designed, it was nearly impossible to support the weight needed to handle cooling and heating equipment, thus making such additions unfeasible.

The cutout proved to be the stadium's signature element. It even earned a cameo in the opening credits of the TV show "Dallas."

25 Drew Pearson was a quarterback in college at the University of Tulsa. No NFL team took him in the 1973 draft, and that was when the draft stretched 17 rounds. Still, the Packers, Steelers, and Cowboys all offered to sign him.

Dallas had the lowest offer, but the best perks.

No, not catching passes from Roger Staubach, although that, too, would become part of the deal. The deciding factor was a $150 bonus and a moonlighting gig of loading 18-wheelers for about triple the minimum wage.

Seven receivers were ahead of Pearson on the depth chart when he arrived. But he was smart enough to stay after practices to get in extra work with Staubach. They developed such a great rapport that Staubach persuaded Schramm to give Pearson $500 so that he could give up the side job and focus solely on catching passes.

After spending the first half of his rookie season returning kicks, Pearson moved into the starting lineup as a receiver. Dallas went 5-1 in his six starts. He would remain a fixture for the rest of Staubach's career and through Danny White's greatest years.

Pearson cracked the 1,000-yard mark twice. Another year he had 870 yards receiving, but it was still enough to lead the NFL. When a car accident ended his playing career after the 1983 season, Pearson had the most catches (489) and most receiving yards (7,822) in team history.

The hallmark of his career wasn't gaudy numbers. It was big plays. When the stakes were high, Staubach and White always looked for No. 88, and he usually delivered. That's why when the Hall of Fame voters put together their All-Decade team for the 1970s, the first-team receivers were Pittsburgh's Lynn Swann and Pearson. And while it took way too long, Pearson eventually made it to the Ring of Honor in 2011, becoming perhaps the last player coached by Tom Landry to get added to the shrine by Jerry Jones.

Now let's review some of Pearson's big plays.

His highlight reel includes an 83-yard, fourth-quarter touchdown to beat the Rams in his first playoff game (1973), a 50-yard game-winning touchdown against Washington on Thanksgiving the following year, and two touchdown catches in the final 3:40 to cap a comeback on the road in Atlanta and send the Cowboys to the NFC Championship game in White's first postseason.

Missing anything? Oh, yeah—the 50-yard pass Staubach hurled his way in the final 20 seconds of a 1975 playoff game in Minnesota.

The ball was underthrown, but Pearson managed to get free of cornerback Nate Wright (push? what push?) and somehow snatch the ball between his right elbow and hip for a 17-14 victory that helped propel Dallas to its third Super Bowl.

Football history included plenty of other last-second bombs that hit their mark, but this one forever found a place in sports lexicon thanks to Staubach's postgame quip: "I closed my eyes and said a Hail Mary."

26 The Super Bowl following the 1977 season was supposed to be decided by the matchup between the Denver Broncos' "Orange Crush" defense and a high-powered Dallas offense featuring Roger Staubach, Tony Dorsett, and Drew Pearson.

Instead, Doomsday II stole the show.

The Dallas D forced eight turnovers—four interceptions and four fumbles. They piled up four sacks. Denver quarterbacks managed just eight completions. It was far more of a whipping than the 27-10 final score indicates.

With nobody putting up big numbers on offense, the temptation might've been to give the MVP award to the entire defense. But logic dictated a single defender should get it . . . only, which one?

Although Randy Hughes intercepted a pass and recovered two fumbles and fellow defensive back Aaron Kyle had one of each, voters were smitten by the relentless pressure from the defensive line. They could've chosen defensive end Harvey Martin (who had two sacks) or defensive tackle Randy White (who had one). The voting was so divided that both ended up being named MVP. It marked the third Super Bowl in which the standout player came from the defense. It's happened only twice since.

This odd decision often appears on lists of worst or most questionable Super Bowl MVPs, but history shows they were worthy choices. Martin was that season's NFL Defensive Player of the Year and would go on to be a second-team All-Decade pick. White, who turned twenty-five that day, was headed for the Ring of Honor and Hall of Fame. (He already had the nickname "Manster," given to him by Charlie Waters because he considered White to be half-man, half-monster.)

White and Martin appeared on the cover of the next issue of *Sports Illustrated* under the headline, "Yippeee!" This was before the era of Super Bowl MVPs going to Disney World. Instead, they went to New York, where each got his own Thunderbird.

Odds are, that was an audible—and a smart one. In January 1978, only a fool would've told Harvey Martin and Randy White that they had to share a car.

27 Leon Lett spent 10 seasons on the Cowboys. Nicknamed the "Big Cat" because of how well he moved for someone his size, he was a key part of a defensive line that helped Dallas win three Super Bowls. He also made the Pro Bowl twice.

So you might think his overall body of work would overcome his two high-profile blunders, especially considering the first came during a Super Bowl victory and the second came in a season that ended with another Super Bowl title.

If so, you'd be thinking wrong.

Lett's first unforgettable gaffe came in the fourth quarter of a Super Bowl rout of Buffalo. Having already KO'd Bills quarterback Jim Kelly, the Cowboys feasted on backup Frank Reich. He fumbled at the Dallas 35-yard line, and Lett took off running with the ball. Steps away from the end zone, he slowed to watch himself on the JumboTron and began lifting the ball in celebration. What he didn't realize was that Buffalo's never-say-die receiver Don Beebe was chasing him. Beebe popped the ball loose just in time to keep Lett from carrying it into the end zone. That prevented two Super Bowl records: Lett would've had the longest fumble return for a touchdown, and the Cowboys would've had the most points. Instead, Lett and Beebe earned roles in one of the most famous Super Bowl blooper video clips, and Dallas still coasted to a 52-17 victory.

While the Super Bowl is an unofficial national holiday, Thanksgiving Day is a real one, and another huge audience was tuned in that day in 1993 to watch the reigning champion Cowboys face the Miami Dolphins. Even casual observers at family gatherings became more interested, because a rare November snowstorm turned Texas Stadium's green plastic turf white. In the coldest regular-season home game in team history, Dallas led, 14-13, with 15 seconds left when Miami's Pete Stoyanovich lined up for a 41-yard field goal, a long one under the circumstances. Dallas's Jimmie Jones blocked the kick, and the ball was spinning harmlessly on the icy turf. The Dolphins couldn't touch it and the Cowboys knew better than to try, because the ball would be dead as soon as it stopped moving. Correction—everyone knew it but Lett. He charged toward the ball, slipped, and slid right into the ball at the 7-yard line.

What was supposed to be a dead ball was suddenly alive, and Miami's Jeff Dellenbach won the race to grab it at the 1-yard line. Given another chance, and a shorter kick, Stoyanovich made it. This would prove to be the final home loss for Jimmy Johnson and the last loss for the '93 Cowboys on their way to a second straight title.

28 Jay Novacek arrived in Dallas in 1990, the same year as Emmitt Smith and the year after Troy Aikman. The difference was that Novacek wasn't a draftee; he was part of a breed of players known as "Plan B free agents," a precursor to the system in place now.

His signing wasn't exactly a big deal, either.

Novacek had been in the NFL for five seasons, all with the Cardinals, and had a whopping six starts. He'd scored eight touchdowns in 63 games—about once every eight games. The Cowboys were so unsure of what they were getting that they also acquired Rob Awalt, who'd shared the tight end job with Novacek in Arizona.

Yet when Novacek slipped into his No. 84 jersey, he and the guy wearing No. 8 just seemed to click.

It was all about trust. Aikman knew that if he put the ball in a certain place, Novacek would be there to squeeze it. The best example was a 23-yard pass that turned into the first touchdown of the first Super Bowl of the Triplets era, tying the game at 7 and helping calm whatever nerves the upstart Cowboys were feeling. (Novacek also scored Dallas's first touchdown in the era's third Super Bowl win, doing so just a month after back surgery.)

Over six seasons in Dallas, Novacek averaged 3.6 catches per game. That may not seem like much, but when you think about all the handoffs to Smith and all the passes to Michael Irvin, there weren't many opportunities for anybody else.

The big thing about Novacek's production is how often those catches came on third down, gaining just enough yards for a new set of downs. He was so good at moving the chains that he made five straight Pro Bowls despite stats that look ordinary compared to today's tight ends. (He averaged 10.5 yards per catch, thus averaging enough for a first down every time.)

Speaking of the difference between generations, Novacek was 6-foot-4 and 234 pounds—about two inches and 30 pounds smaller than Jason Witten. Novacek had been a quarterback in high school and a decathlete and pole vaulter in college. He was far more of a receiver than a blocker, but considering the caliber of the rest of the guys on the offensive line, he proved to be exactly the kind of tight end that unit needed. His hands were so reliable that he served as the holder on extra points and field goals.

Back problems ended his career at thirty-three. In retrospect, his departure was the beginning of the end for the Triplets. Not that his absence triggered the demise; it was just the first reminder that guys can't stay in their prime forever.

29 In 1961, the Cowboys were so desperate for help at linebacker that they hired a guy who'd spent the prior year working at a gas station in West Virginia.

Bringing in Chuck Howley proved to be a brilliant move.

A first-round pick by Chicago in 1958, Howley left the NFL after two seasons because of a bum knee. Then he played in a college alumni game and told a friend he was thinking about a comeback. That friend was Don Healy, a defensive tackle who started every game for Dallas in 1960 and would do so again in '61. Healy alerted the front office that Howley was interested, and the Cowboys' second-chance hotel had another resident.

Dallas gave Chicago two future draft picks for Howley and ended up with a stalwart for the next 13 years.

Howley made first-team All-Pro five straight seasons, from 1966 to 1970. And then, in the final game of the 1970 season, he pulled off a feat that's unlikely ever to be duplicated.

Howley was voted MVP of the Super Bowl following the 1970 season even though the Cowboys lost, 16-13, to the Baltimore Colts on a field goal in the closing seconds. It was such a sloppy game—it's remembered as "The Blunder Bowl" because of all the penalties and turnovers—that nobody really shined. So Howley's two interceptions and a forced fumble loomed large. (He also became the first defensive player to be Super Bowl MVP.)

Super Bowls clearly brought out the best in Howley, as he had another interception and a fumble recovery in the next Super Bowl, the first one the Cowboys ever won.

Howley became the fourth player inducted into the Ring of Honor. However, his jersey, No. 54, went back into circulation and returned to prominence with Randy White.

30 Tex and Tom. Jerry and Jimmy. It's hard to imagine one without the other. As far as players go, there may be no two guys more closely associated in Cowboys lore than Cliff Harris and Charlie Waters.

Both arrived in 1970, Waters as a third-round pick from Clemson University and Harris as an undrafted free agent from Ouachita Baptist College in Arkansas.

Cliff wore No. 41 and picked up the nickname "Captain Crash" because of his reckless hitting. Charlie wore No. 43 and was the rah-rah leader, the guy who kept saying, "You gotta believe," as a guest analyst during the radio broadcast of what proved to be the final miraculous comeback of Roger Staubach's career. (You'll read more about that game later in the book.)

Their rookie year, Harris started at free safety, and Waters was his backup. Then the military called Harris away, and Waters took over. Harris returned in time to play in the Super Bowl, but Waters started.

Harris reclaimed the free safety job the next year, while Waters bounced around as a backup at strong safety and cornerback. In 1975, Tom Landry finally put them together at the two safety spots. Dallas went back to the Super Bowl that season and three times in four years.

Harris was named to the NFL's All-Decade team for the 1970s and joined the Ring of Honor in 2004. Waters's nine postseason interceptions are tied for the most in NFL history.

31 In 1989, the Minnesota Vikings stunned everyone by trading so much to get a single player, Herschel Walker.

Their premise was somewhat sound. They believed they were a running back away from winning it all, and that was something the franchise had never done despite four Super Bowl trips. So if Walker could put them over the top, overpaying a little was worth it.

Well, they overpaid by a lot. And they didn't win it all. Instead, the Cowboys parlayed their bundle of assets into the foundation of their run of three Super Bowl titles in four years. The confluence of those things is why this is widely viewed as one of the biggest heists among all pro sports swaps.

In October 1989, the Cowboys were well on their way to the worst season since their debut. They were already 0-5 when Jimmy Johnson brought up the idea of trading their best player, Walker.

On face value, it was preposterous. Again, Walker was their *best* player. But they also weren't going anywhere with him. Johnson, fresh from college football, wanted to build through the draft and knew that giving up a commodity others wanted (Walker) would bring in what he wanted.

The Cleveland Browns offered a handful of first- and second-round picks. But why accept the first offer? Johnson called Mike Lynn of the Vikings, and they struck the following swap:

- To Minnesota: Walker, Dallas's third- and 10th-round picks in 1990, and a third-round pick in '91.
- To Dallas: Minnesota's first-, second-, and sixth-round picks in 1990, running back Darrin Nelson, defensive end Alex Stewart, cornerback Issiac Holt, and linebackers Jesse Solomon and David Howard.

Plus, there was a caveat, the wrinkle that changed everything (and the reason Johnson immediately dubbed the deal "The Great Train Robbery"): if the Cowboys cut any of those players before February 1, 1990, Dallas would get an additional pick from Minnesota.

The Vikings surely thought that the rebuilding Cowboys needed all the live bodies they could get. This was Lynn's major mistake. All along, Johnson considered those players as extra draft picks. Right away, he dealt the disgruntled Nelson for two choices and cut Stewart, guaranteeing at least one more pick from Minnesota. Once Lynn realized Johnson's master plan, they worked out another deal to settle things once and for all.

Johnson later made so many deals with those picks that it's impossible to trace it all. But it's easy to say that the Walker trade yielded Emmitt Smith, Darren Woodson, Kevin Smith, and Russell Maryland.

A postscript to the deal is that not only did Walker fail to put the Vikings over the top, he later returned to Dallas.

32 George Teague went through two stints in Dallas, a one-year stay in 1996 and then a return engagement from 1998 to 2001.

Of his 71 games with the Cowboys, the one folks talk about the most occurred on September 24, 2000.

That day's drama began when 49ers receiver Terrell Owens decided to punctuate a touchdown not in the end zone, but atop the Cowboys' star logo at midfield. He spread his arms wide and tilted his head back, then jogged to the sideline. Emmitt Smith matched fire with fire, taking his own touchdown celebration to the 50-yard line, dropping to a knee, and slamming the ball onto the logo.

That only raised the stakes for T.O.

When Owens scored again, he returned to center stage. Just as he slammed the ball down—à la Smith—in came Teague, delivering the blow almost everyone wanted to see.

Owens was still crouched when Teague drove into him with a shoulder, sending the receiver tumbling. Teague never lost his balance. In the immediate aftermath, an offensive lineman tried taking out Teague but missed, and Owens went back to finish his pose on the star.

It's important to note that Owens was rubbing in a 41-17 lead and that temperatures on the turf that sunny afternoon were way too high to keep emotions in check. But Teague's

George Teague is best remembered for his KO of T.O. But Teague's favorite picture of his Dallas days is this one, from the first home game after the September 11 terrorist attacks. (AP Photo/Tim Sharp)

response wasn't spontaneous. He had already decided to retaliate if Owens went back to midfield.

Almost exactly a year later, in the Cowboys' first home game following the September 11 terrorist attacks, Teague—who grew up on military bases—grabbed a U.S. flag from someone in the tunnel and ran out waving it proudly. A picture of that scene hangs in a prominent spot at AT&T Stadium. (Teague also displays that picture, not the one of the T.O. takedown, in his office and home.)

33 Let's properly set the stage for this.

This was a matchup of NFL giants. The Cowboys were playing in their fifth Super Bowl of the decade and came in as the reigning champs. The Steelers were playing in their third Super Bowl of the decade, having won the previous two—one of them against Dallas. The winner of this game would become the first team to win three Super Bowls and could claim the title of the NFL's "Team of the 1970s."

With a few minutes left in the third quarter, the Cowboys are trailing, 21-14. But they are closing in on the tying touchdown. It is third-and-3 from the Pittsburgh 10-yard line.

When Staubach receives the play in the huddle, he's so surprised that he calls timeout to discuss it with Landry. Should they really use a goal-line formation this far from the end zone?

Landry said that was exactly what he wanted to do. And, sure enough, the play worked to perfection—at least from a design standpoint.

Here's how Verne Lundquist described it on the Cowboys' radio broadcast of the game:

> *"Roger back to throw. Has a man open in the end zone! Caught! Touchdown, SMITH! Dropped in the end zone! Jackie Smith, over himself. Oh, bless his heart, he's got to be the sickest man in America. Aww, Jackie was so wide open in the end zone it was in-CREDIBLE. And he could not hang onto the ball."*

To this day, Staubach insists the pass was a tad low and a tick behind Smith. He also says it was thrown soft with a wobble. Staubach added that he felt the timing of the play was thrown off because he was used to running it from the goal line, not the 10.

There's no justifying it, though. It was just a horrible drop, especially when you consider that Smith went into that game with the most catches of any tight end in NFL history. That's what got him to the Hall of Fame.

Smith caught 480 passes over 15 years with the St. Louis Cardinals. He played in 12 games for Dallas in the 1978 regular season and didn't catch a single pass. However, he did have three catches in the first round of the playoffs, including the game-tying touchdown in the third quarter against Atlanta. So you could say he helped the Cowboys get to that Super Bowl. But we'll never know how that game might have turned out if only he'd held onto that crucial pass.

34 The last few spots on an NFL roster are always in flux. Out of training camp, they often go to players with marginal skills at their preferred position but with enough versatility to contribute on special teams. It helps if they match maximum effort on the field with doing all the right things off the field, such as watching film and studying the playbook.

That's the formula that Bill Bates followed to catch Tom Landry's eye. And once he made the roster, Bates stayed there for 15 years.

"If we had 11 players on the field who played as hard as Bill Bates does and did their homework like he does, we'd be almost impossible to beat," Landry said.

In Bates's second season, 1984, his special teams play was so outstanding that the NFL created a Pro Bowl spot just to give it to him. He was also a four-time winner of the team's Bob Lilly Award for being a fan favorite.

Bates actually started 47 times at safety for Landry, but never again once Jimmy Johnson took over. Still, Bates's work on special teams and as a backup on defense helped Dallas win three Super Bowl titles in the 1990s and helped keep him on the roster through 1997.

35 Daryl Johnston's nickname was so catchy that he even heard "Mooooose" calls on the road.

His popularity stemmed not from what he did with the ball, but form the way he performed when others had the ball—primarily Troy Aikman and Emmitt Smith. He was such a good human shield that the NFL added a fullback position to the Pro Bowl roster to include him on the squad in 1993 and '94.

But before we focus on his selflessness, let's go over the nickname's origin story.

Babe Laufenberg hung it on Johnston in the early 1990s, when Laufenberg was a backup quarterback. He saw a group of running backs—small guys, mostly—standing together and was struck by how much the 6-foot-2 Johnston towered above his peers. To Laufenberg, Johnston looked like a moose infiltrating a herd of deer. So from that point on, Johnston became "Moose."

In an offense filled with glitzy headliners, Johnston was a perfect complement, a bruising, blend-in-with-the-crowd kind of guy. Those headliners loved and appreciated his contribution, especially once his playing style caught up to him in the form of neck problems that forced him to retire in 1999.

Aikman called Johnston "as good playing his position as anyone has been playing their position." And when Smith became the NFL's career rushing champion, his one regret was not having Johnston open the hole for him. There was some solace, though: Johnston was on the sideline as a broadcaster.

36 Larry Brown was the right person in the right place at the right time. Twice. In a Super Bowl, no less.

Brown came into the league as a 12th-round pick, then became the rare Cowboys rookie to start at cornerback. He was part of the secondary that helped win championship in 1992 and '93, with Brown even snagging an interception in the first of those Super Bowls.

In the Super Bowl following the 1995 season—Dallas's most recent trip to the title game—Brown was the beneficiary of two overthrown passes by Pittsburgh's Neil O'Donnell.

The first came midway through the third quarter, with the Steelers moving toward a potential game-tying touchdown. Brown caught a pass intended for Ernie Mills, and his return led to a touchdown by Emmitt Smith that stretched Dallas's lead to 20-7.

The Steelers clawed back to within 20-17 and had the ball again late in the fourth quarter, when O'Donnell's pass to Andre Hastings wound up in Brown's hands. Once again, his return led to a Smith touchdown, this one sealing the victory.

Brown became the first cornerback to be Super Bowl MVP, and one of the least likely. This career highlight also came in the wake of a personal tragedy. In November, his newborn son—born more than three months premature—died after just 10 weeks.

37 Imagine a player who scored more touchdowns than Michael Irvin, scored more often per catch than Terrell Owens and Jerry Rice, and who averaged more yards per catch than Randy Moss.

Now imagine that the same guy averaged more yards per punt return than Deion Sanders.

That's how dynamic "Bullet" Bob Hayes was.

Hayes made an impact from the start. In his very first game, he caught two passes: a 36-yard gain and a 45-yard touchdown.

In his next game, he caught another 45-yard touchdown and ran 11 yards for another score.

Pro football had never seen anything like his blend of raw speed and football prowess. By the end of his rookie season, he'd become the team's first 1,000-yard receiver, and, for the first time, Dallas avoided a losing record. He also led the NFL in touchdown catches.

In his second season, Hayes upped his receiving total to 1,232 yards, a figure that remained the club's single-season record until Michael Irvin topped it in 1991. Hayes again led the league in touchdown catches, and the Cowboys came within a sliver of reaching the first Super Bowl.

In 1970, when the Cowboys reached their first Super Bowl, Hayes led the NFL in yards per catch. He did so again the next year, when the Cowboys finally won it all. That championship gave him perhaps the sporting world's coolest jewelry collection: an Olympic gold medal and a Super Bowl ring.

He's still the only person with one of each.

There was a notion that you couldn't overthrow Hayes. He also wasn't particular about who was throwing it. He caught a 95-yard touchdown from Don Meredith, an 89-yarder from Craig Morton, and an 85-yarder from Roger Staubach.

Defenses scrambled to find a way to contain him. Eventually, the combination of rules changes and Father Time slowed Hayes's production.

His legacy was tarnished by a prison sentence that was later overturned. But the man who first conditioned Cowboys fans to expect No. 22 to reach the end zone (long before Emmitt Smith was even born) eventually got his due. Hayes was inducted into the Ring of Honor in 2001. He died a year later at age fifty-nine. The Hall of Fame finally made room for him in 2009.

38 Larry Allen rarely spoke—not to reporters, not to foes, and hardly even to teammates or coaches.

He just blocked. And blocked. And blocked.

Larry Allen (73) mauled anyone who tried getting by him to the Cowboys' backfield. Yet once a play ended, he turned quiet. This is about as demonstrative as he got. (AP Photo/David Phillip)

No matter where he played on the line—whether he was at the line of scrimmage, pulling on a sweep, or charging down the field looking for someone to hit—Allen was a nightmare to play against.

Allen was the best pick in the years after Jimmy Johnson left the draft room, when Jerry Jones and his buddy Larry Lacewell controlled picks. They spent a second-round pick on the big guy out of a little school (Sonoma State University in Northern California), and everyone marveled at him from the start.

There aren't many good statistics to quantify the contribution of offensive linemen, but here's one to consider: Emmitt Smith was already a three-time rushing champion before Allen joined the Cowboys. In Allen's first season as a starter, Smith ran for the most yards in his career. It's fair to say that Smith's path to becoming the NFL's all-time rushing champion was paved in large part by No. 73.

Allen's 10 Pro Bowls and six selections to All-Pro squads are nice, but the real mark of excellence is his dual All-Decade honors. He went into the Ring of Honor in 2011 and the Hall of Fame in 2013.

39 Dan Bailey has been so ridiculously good in the first five seasons of his career that he could have missed his first four kicks in 2016 and still have been the most accurate kicker in league history.

Through 2015, Bailey made 144 of 159 attempts. That's an accuracy rate of 90.57 percent. Second-best on the all-time list is 87.84 percent.

(Quick bit of context here: Modern-day kickers are more accurate than their predecessors by almost ridiculous margins. Fourteen of the top 17 on the NFL's all-time accuracy list were active in 2015, and two others retired in recent years. The only one who's been out of the league for a decade happens to be a former Cowboy, Mike Vanderjagt; funny thing is, he'd be higher on the career list if not for a career-worst 72.2 percent season in Dallas.)

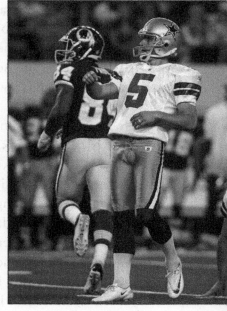

Dan Bailey has been "Mr. Automatic" since joining the Cowboys in 2011. (AP Photo/ LM Otero)

As a senior at Oklahoma State University, Bailey won the Lou Groza Award as college football's best kicker, yet he wasn't drafted. Free to sign anywhere, he chose Dallas and in the third game of his career made six field goals, providing all the points in an 18-16 victory over the Redskins. Bailey has been piling up streaks, milestones, and records ever since. Whether it's a long kick, a high-stakes kick, or a long kick with high stakes, Bailey is always a good bet to come through.

And when it comes to extra points, he's been absolutely perfect: 204 of 204.

40 His driver's license said Wilford Jones. Generations of Cowboys fans—and Cowboys haters—knew him as "Crazy Ray."

His connection to the team started in the Cotton Bowl in 1962. He started out selling pennants, using a whistle to grab attention. That's how he picked up his first nickname, "Whistling Ray."

He fine-tuned his shtick for years, working his way onto the sidelines riding a stick pony in his signature get-up. TV cameras loved him, and so did kids of all ages. Among his signature stunts were pretending to gun down the Redskins' mascot and using items bearing the logo of the opposing team to wipe sweat off his forehead.

"Crazy Ray" was never on the team's payroll, although he did get an all-access pass and a parking pass to home games. He was also a regular at Super Bowls.

Jones died in 2007. He was seventy-six.

STARTER LEVEL

Congrats on making it through your rookie days. You've earned your way into the starting lineup. The questions in this section are a little tougher, requiring deeper knowledge. We also introduce a new type of challenge—the multi-layered question. Good luck.

1 How did the Cowboys become known as "America's Team"? *Answer on page 65.*

2 How many Hall of Famers are enshrined primarily because of their accomplishments with the Cowboys? (Bonus: Name them all.) *Answer on page 67.*

3 Between Tom Landry and Jason Garrett, the job of head coach of the Cowboys was a bit of a revolving door. *Answer on page 70.*
   • How many coaches have the Cowboys had, including Landry and Garrett?
   • Can you list them in order?
   • How about listing them in order of their win total?

4 Who was the first starting quarterback in Cowboys history? *Answer on page 71.*

5 Name the player who started at quarterback for the Cowboys in their first Super Bowl and started against them in another Super Bowl. *Answer on page 73.*

6 In recent years, Cowboys fans have became accustomed to the division titles coming down to the season finale. It also happened in 1979, when the Redskins came to Texas Stadium for what turned out to be a wild, dramatic Dallas victory. Harvey Martin celebrated by visiting the Washington locker room and delivering this item. *Answer on page 76.*

7 Who am I? *Answer on page 79.*
- I picked up the nickname "The Mad Bomber" in my first training camp, because a pass intended for a receiver instead hit Tom Landry's coaching tower.
- Tired of being a backup, I forced my way out of town by sucker-punching Roger Staubach during training camp in 1976.
- I'm best remembered for my first NFL game: replacing Staubach on Thanksgiving Day in 1974 and throwing two late touchdown passes to beat the Redskins, 24-23.

8 The most regular-season games the Cowboys have played against any opponent is 110; it's been done against two teams. However, when you add in playoff games, they've faced one of those teams a couple more times. Name that most-frequent foe. *Answer on page 81.*

9 Which team has Dallas beaten the most times? (Hint: It's not the same team as from the previous question. It's the other one referenced in that question.) *Answer on page 84.*

10 OK, let's shift to only the postseason. Which team has Dallas played most often in the playoffs? *Answer on page 89.*

11 Which team has Dallas beaten most often in the playoffs? *Answer on page 91.*

12 Now let's flip it around: which team has beaten Dallas the most often in the regular season? *Answer on page 93.*

13 Which team has beaten Dallas the most often in the play-offs? *Answer on page 96.*

14 The Cowboys have had three owners. You've already answered a question about the founder. And you certainly know that Jerry Jones is the current owner. But what about the guy in between—what's his name? *Answer on page 98.*

15 The Cowboys won a single game in the first year of the Jerry Jones-Jimmy Johnson era. Who'd they beat? *Answer on page 100.*

16 The heart and soul of Tom Landry's Flex defense was the middle linebacker, particularly _____, who combined a fearless playing style with intense leadership. *Answer on page 102.*

17 Who am I? *Answer on page 105.*

• Not just a Cowboy, I also was a cowboy; a horse trailer was the signing bonus for my rookie contract.

• Among the many lines I'm known for was this response to a question about whether Tom Landry ever smiles: "No, but then I've only been around here for nine years."

• My good buddy Don Meredith quipped: "If you needed four yards, you'd give the ball to [me] and he'd get you four yards. If you needed 20 yards, you'd give the ball to [me] and he'd get you four yards."

18 Who was the last first-round draft pick of the Tom Landry-Tex Schramm-Gil Brandt era? *Answer on page 106.*

19 Which former player wrote the thinly veiled novel *North Dallas Forty,* about his time with the Cowboys? *Answer on page 109.*

20 Since Emmitt Smith left, which Cowboy has rushed for the most yards? (Hint: the answer is the same for most yards in a single game, a single season, and the entire tenure.) *Answer on page 111.*

21 Two of the most dominant defensive ends in team history wore No. 94. In the 1990s, it was future Hall of Famer _____. In the 2000s, it was _____. *Answer on page 112.*

22 The Cowboys went 0-11-1 in their debut season, 1960. What team did they tie for their first nonloss? *Answer on page 115.*

23 The Cowboys' first win came in 1961. Who'd they beat? *Answer on page 116.*

24 Tony Romo wears No. 9 in honor of which fictional sports hero? *Answer on page 117.*

25 Before becoming "America's Team," the Cowboys had a less flattering nickname. What was it? *Answer on page 119.*

26 In 2007, Ron Springs needed a new kidney to extend his life. The donor was former teammate _____. *Answer on page 120.*

27 Who am I? *Answer on page 122.*
- I won the Outland Trophy as the best interior lineman in college football as a senior but wasn't taken until the 11th round of the draft.
- Teams ignored me because of my military commitment. I was supposed to be in the Air Force for eight

years but was released after four years, having flown missions in the first Gulf War.

- I arrived in the NFL in time to win three Super Bowls with the Cowboys. I played a total of nine seasons.

28 Of all the Cowboys' head coaches, which came to Dallas with the most wins as an NFL head coach? *Answer on page 123.*

29 Several head coaches went on to be head coach of other NFL teams after leaving Dallas. Which went on to win the most games? *Answer on page 125.*

30 Troy Aikman was hurt and sat out the first playoff game of his career. Who started in his place? *Answer on page 127.*

STARTER LEVEL – ANSWERS

1 By winning, right?

It certainly starts there.

By having dynamic personalities on and off the field?

Well, that helped.

Because of the cheerleaders?

Didn't hurt, either.

Snazzy uniforms? A unique home stadium? Playing in a bunch of Super Bowls just as the NFL's popularity was taking off?

If you haven't already guessed, the answer is rooted in all of the above. But it's not the complete answer.

The phrase comes from Bob Ryan, a producer for NFL Films. He needed a title for the 1978 season wrap-up video. Dallas's loss to Pittsburgh in the Super Bowl prevented options such as *Back-to-Back Titles* or *Three-Time Champs*. So he had to be more creative.

As he watched that season's games, something struck him: Everywhere the Cowboys went, huge crowds cheered them on. They'd gone far beyond local or regional favorites; they'd become a national sensation. They were . . . well, "America's Team."

Here's how the name is introduced, in the opening of the video, as announced by the deep voice of NFL Films' famed narrator John Facenda:

> *They are the Notre Dame of professional football,*
> *a national team whose popularity extends from coast to coast.*

No matter where the Cowboys travel, there are always fans to greet them.
Their players are heroes to the young,
and their success and style has gained them a following across the United States.
They appear on television so often that their faces are as familiar to the public as presidents and movie stars.
They are the Dallas Cowboys: America's Team.

The name obviously stuck, much to the chagrin of Tom Landry. He felt it gave opponents even more motivation to try beating the Cowboys. He was right, too. When the Houston Oilers beat the Cowboys on Thanksgiving Day in 1979, their coach, Bum Phillips, said: "If they're America's team, I guess we must be Texas's team—and that's better."

Tex Schramm didn't care about any of that. He knew marketing gold when he heard it and took full advantage, even having the Texas Stadium PA voice introduce the Cowboys as "America's Team" as they ran onto the field.

Every so often, a team will rise in popularity and try to make a claim of now being "America's Team". Yet no matter how high they stack TV ratings, merchandise sales, and Twitter followers, their case is built on a faulty foundation. "America's Team" isn't a title that can be passed around, like boxing's heavyweight crown or track's honorific of world's fastest man. It's a nickname that was bestowed upon a particular team at a particular time, and it clicked with the masses. You can change that no more than you can change what happened when that pass hit Jackie Smith between the 8 and the 1 in the end zone of the Super Bowl featured in the video that started the whole "America's Team" phenomenon.

2 The Pro Football Hall of Fame's website includes a roster of honorees by franchise. Under each franchise is a list of every Hall of Famer connected with the club. This means that people involved with multiple teams get listed in multiple places. For instance, Emmitt Smith is listed with both the Cowboys and the Cardinals, and Tony Dorsett is listed with the Cowboys and the Broncos.

Yet each person's name is in bold on the club where they "made the major part of their primary contribution."

The Dallas list includes 15 people in bold type: 13 players, a coach, and an executive.

NAME	SEASONS IN DALLAS	HOF INDUCTION
Bob Lilly	1961-74	1980
Roger Staubach	1969-79	1985
Tom Landry	1960-88	1990
Tex Schramm	1960-89	1991
Tony Dorsett	1977-87	1994
Randy White	1975-88	1994
Mel Renfro	1964-77	1996
Troy Aikman	1989-2000	2006
Rayfield Wright	1967-79	2006
Michael Irvin	1988-99	2007
Bob Hayes	1965-74	2009
Emmitt Smith	1990-2002	2010
Deion Sanders*^	1995-99	2011
Larry Allen	1994-2005	2013
Charles Haley*	1992-96	2015

* Sanders is listed in bold for both Dallas and Atlanta, as he spent five years with each. Haley is listed in bold for Dallas and San Francisco; although he played more seasons with the 49ers, he won three of his five Super Bowls with the Cowboys.

^ Sanders is the only member of this list who is not in the Ring of Honor.

The Hall of Fame includes seven more players in regular type on Dallas's online honor roll. Thus, these guys played for the Cowboys, but not in their greatest days. They are:

NAME	SEASON(S) IN DALLAS	HOF INDUCTION
Forrest Gregg	1971	1977
Lance Alworth	1971-72	1978
Herb Adderley	1970-72	1980
Mike Ditka	1969-72	1988
Jackie Smith	1978	1994
Tommy McDonald	1964	1998
Bill Parcells	2003-06	2013

Take a closer look at the years of induction, and you'll see how poorly represented the Cowboys are, at least in comparison to how dominant they were, particularly in the 1970s.

Plays like this carried Mel Renfro (20) to the Hall of Fame. His 52 interceptions are easily the most in team history. (AP Photo)

In the 25 years after Lilly was enshrined, the only teammates who joined him were Staubach and Renfro. White and Dorsett went in, too, but both began their careers after Lilly retired.

The oversights led to talk of a Hall of Fame bias against the Cowboys. Whatever you think of conspiracy theories, this one had its merits.

Five Super Bowls in the 1970s and only five players in the Hall as of 2005? It was out of whack in comparison to the number of players enshrined from less-successful teams and out of whack compared to other dominant teams. Put another way, it was like only the Cowboys were being punished for having had a lot of great players at the same time.

The weirdest part is that the same voters who choose Hall of Famers also choose the All-Decade teams. So the same people who considered Cliff Harris, Harvey Martin, Ralph Neely, and Drew Pearson as being among the best of their generation at that time were later deemed not to have been as outstanding when given more time to think about it. This makes sense, to a certain extent. Otherwise, making the All-Decade Team would essentially mean making the Hall. But it still feels unbalanced.

The tide has turned in recent years. Just when the stars of the 1990s-era clubs became eligible, more of their Dallas football forefathers started getting a closer look. Some changes in the voting process helped, too. The bottom line is that things have improved, and, perhaps, more of the people who turned the Cowboys into "America's Team" will get another look. If the seniors committee is in need of any candidates, a good place to start is the seven guys who are in the Ring of Honor but not in the Hall of Fame:

- Pearson
- Harris

- Lee Roy Jordan
- Darren Woodson
- Don Meredith
- Don Perkins
- Chuck Howley

3 Just like Tom Landry used to have the unique distinction of being the only coach in Cowboys history, Jerry Jones has the unique distinction of having fired and/or hired every coach in Cowboys history. His fingerprints are all over this list, for better or worse.

Garrett is the eighth coach in team history. His tenure is already the longest since Landry's. Everyone else lasted between two and five seasons.

Here they are, in chronological order:

COACH	SEASONS	TENURE
Tom Landry	1960-88	29 seasons
Jimmy Johnson	1989-93	5 seasons
Barry Switzer	1994-97	4 seasons
Chan Gailey	1998-99	2 seasons
Dave Campo	2000-02	3 seasons
Bill Parcells	2003-06	4 seasons
Wade Phillips	2007-mid 2010	3.5 seasons
Jason Garrett	mid 2010-present	5.5 seasons and counting

The list becomes more interesting when we sort it based on how many regular-season games the Cowboys won on their watch.

COACH	WINS
Landry	250
Garrett	45
Johnson	44
Switzer	40
Parcells	34
Phillips	34
Gailey	18
Campo	15

Before we leave this subject, let's filter these guys in a way that's even more important than regular-season wins—postseason wins.

That last line was a bit of a litmus test. If you sighed, groaned, or said unprintable things, then you have a pretty good grasp of Cowboys history. Because the cruel reality is that the drop-off on this list is pretty ugly, a reminder of how many lean years this once-proud franchise has put their fans through:

COACH	POSTSEASON WINS
Landry	20 (2 Super Bowls)
Johnson	7 (2 Super Bowls)
Switzer	5 (1 Super Bowl)
Garrett	1
Phillips	1
Campo	0
Gailey	0
Parcells	0

4 This sounds like a joke, but it's absolutely true: the first snap in franchise history was taken by a thirty-year-old, 5-foot-7, 160-pound lawyer who'd been coaxed out of retirement.

It took 13 tries before he won a game for Dallas. His career record for the Cowboys was 4-21-1.

Now the real zinger. Eddie LeBaron deserves a huge round of applause. He made the most of a tough situation, and Tom Landry appreciated "the Little General" more than anyone.

"We needed a cagey veteran like LeBaron, who could help teach Meredith the tricks of his trade and give us some starting experience until Don and the rest of the team matured," Landry wrote in his autobiography.

Landry knew his expansion team was unlikely to be competitive, so he needed the crucial job of starting quarterback to go to a respected pro. He had to be a steadying influence, someone who wouldn't undermine things by bellyaching about how lousy the club was.

He had to be tough enough to take a pounding and mentally strong enough to know he was just holding down the fort until more help arrived, in the form of Meredith and an influx of talent that club officials knew they'd bring in.

LeBaron checked every box.

As a Marine, LeBaron valiantly served his country in Korea, earning a Bronze Star for bravery and multiple Purple Hearts.

As for football skills, LeBaron made the Pro Bowl three times, including as recently as two seasons before he came to Dallas.

LeBaron played college ball at the University of Pacific, with his first season being the last for legendary college coach Amos Alonzo Stagg. LeBaron was so good as a quarterback, safety, and punter at Pacific that he was inducted into the College Football Hall of Fame. In the NFL, he replaced Sammy Baugh as quarterback in Washington and was named the league's Rookie of the Year in 1952.

LeBaron promised Landry three seasons. He led the NFL in passer rating and made the Pro Bowl in his third season, so he stuck around for another year.

Even after returning to law, LeBaron remained involved in football as a broadcaster for CBS and through work with the league office and the players' association. He was general manager of the Falcons from 1977 to 1982, winning the Executive of the Year award in 1980, then served a few more years in their front office. He was also on the NFL's powerful Competition Committee.

LeBaron's stats as a Cowboy aren't too impressive: over 52 games, he threw 45 touchdowns and 53 interceptions while completing 51.9 percent of his passes. Still, his contribution to team history is worth remembering, both for the novelty of being the first starting quarterback and for how he handled such a difficult role.

LeBaron died in 2015. He was eighty-five.

5 Craig Morton puts it this way: "I was never on the right side of the scoreboard in those Super Bowls. At least I made Tom (Landry) happy once."

Twice, actually, but we'll get to that later.

As his bittersweet quote indicates, Morton had a fascinating, complicated time in Dallas, one filled with highs and lows.

Morton was a first-round pick in 1965, taken fifth overall—right after Dick Butkus and Gale Sayers and seven picks before Joe Namath. A star at the University of California, Morton stood 6-foot-4 and weighed 214 pounds. Unlike LeBaron, Morton looked like a star quarterback, plus he had a rocket arm.

He was brought in to be groomed as the heir to Don Meredith. Sure enough, when Dandy Don retired, Morton took over and led the Cowboys to their first Super Bowl. They won it all the next year.

If it seems like there's a missing element to this narrative, you're right. His name is Roger Staubach.

While Morton was serving his apprenticeship, Staubach was serving his country. Staubach joined the team full-time just as Morton was ascending the throne as the starter. In fact, a dislocated finger kept Morton out of the 1969 opener. Staubach started instead. And won.

Luckily for Morton, Landry was a huge believer in quarterbacks waiting their turn.

Landry saw value in bringing along quarterbacks slowly, making sure his triggermen fully understood the system before he trusted them to implement it in a game. Remember, Meredith spent time as Eddie LeBaron's backup. But Morton also knew Staubach was no typical youngster. (In fact, Staubach was a year older than Morton—to the day. Both were born on February 5.) So when Morton hurt his throwing shoulder, he kept playing. He compensated for that pain by changing his motion and wound up also hurting his elbow.

Even though Morton got the Cowboys over a hump by leading them to the Super Bowl following the 1970 season, he was pretty awful in that game: 12 of 26 for 137 yards and three interceptions. All three interceptions came in the final 8:30, as Dallas let a 13-6 lead dissolve into a 16-13 loss.

Staubach was the only healthy offensive player who didn't see the field that day. On the flight home, Landry promised Staubach that he'd get a chance the next year.

Landry's waffling between Morton and Staubach nearly doomed the Cowboys in 1971. The quarterbacks alternated starts, and then, on Halloween, Landry had them alternate snaps. Dallas lost that day, and Landry realized he had to pick one.

In 1971, Craig Morton (14) was twenty-eight, in his third straight year as the primary starter, and coming off a Super Bowl. So Tom Landry was slow to replace him with Roger Staubach (12). Once the change was made, the Cowboys didn't lose again, winning their first Super Bowl title. (AP Photo/Harold Waters)

Heavy odds seemed to favor Morton. Yet Landry picked Staubach. The Cowboys won every game the rest of the season, including their first Super Bowl title.

Staubach, of course, would keep the job the rest of the decade. Dallas traded Morton to the New York Giants in 1974 for a first-round pick. Morton's first start happened to come against the Cowboys. (Dallas won.) And that draft pick turned out to be Randy White.

The next stop in Morton's career was Denver, starting in 1977. He was terrific that year, getting named the NFL's Comeback Player of the Year while guiding the Broncos to the Super Bowl . . . against the Cowboys. In the big game,

Morton completed as many passes to Dallas players (four interceptions) as he did to guys wearing orange (four completions) before being replaced. This is what he meant by making Landry happy once. (The kicker to this is that one of the key defenders responsible for Morton's horrid stats was none other than White, who earned co-MVP honors in that Super Bowl.)

Morton played 18 seasons in the NFL, lasting to 1982. Cowboys fans may not remember him fondly—if they remember him at all—but Staubach sure does. Ask him about the great quarterbacks in team history, and he'll always mention Morton. For all the statistical feats that Tony Romo has earned, Morton still leads him 1-0 in the crucial category of Super Bowl starts.

Now, about that other time Morton made Landry happy in a Super Bowl.

It goes back to the final moments of the Super Bowl following the 1971 season, the one Staubach won after displacing Morton. To his credit, Morton was never bitter. If he ever complained to a reporter that season, he did so strictly off the record. And as the final seconds counted down, Morton went to Landry, shook his hand, and said, "Congratulations. I'm really happy for you."

6 A black funeral wreath arrived at Cowboys headquarters days before the season finale and was delivered to Harvey Martin's locker. A card attached to the flowers said it was a gift from the Redskins.

Funny, eh? Not to Martin. Not after what had happened in Washington a few weeks earlier. Not with a high-stakes game coming up.

Let's back up to explain the situation.

In mid-November, the Redskins beat the Cowboys by 14 points in Washington; along the way, the Redskins sacked Roger Staubach five times, eventually knocking him out of the game. Yet what really stung was that Washington had an 11-point lead with time running out and couldn't let things be. Coach Jack Pardee stretched the margin of victory with a field goal. The playoff chase was so tight that margin of victory might be a consideration. Still, to the Cowboys, it felt insulting.

Going into the finale, that tight playoff race continued, with Dallas, Washington, and Philadelphia all 10-5. The Cowboys-Redskins winner was guaranteed a playoff spot; odds were good for the loser, but it wasn't guaranteed.

The Cowboys also went into this game with Tony Dorsett sitting out because of an injury. And although they didn't know it, this would be Roger Staubach's final regular-season game.

OK, now the stage is set.

Dallas coughed up a pair of fumbles early on, and Washington capitalized, jumping ahead, 17-0. Then Ron Springs ran for a touchdown, and Preston Pearson made a diving catch in the end zone in the final seconds before halftime, getting the Cowboys within 17-14. The momentum carried over into the third quarter, with Robert Newhouse rushing for the go-ahead touchdown.

Then it was the Redskins' turn to dominate. They kicked a field goal to get close, then broke the game open with a pair of touchdown runs by John Riggins. This included a 66-yarder, which would be the longest of his Hall of Fame career.

Washington got the ball again with about five minutes left and leading, 34-21. Thousands of fans at Texas Stadium became more interested in beating traffic and started heading for their cars. Charlie Waters, who was out with an injury and working as a color commentator on the radio broadcast, kept insisting, "You gotta believe!"

Waters's pal Cliff Harris began the turnaround by causing a fumble that led to a touchdown pass from Staubach to Springs. While that got the Cowboys within six points, all the Redskins needed were a few first downs to drain the clock. However, Larry Cole stuffed Riggins on third-and-2, and Washington had to punt the ball back to Dallas.

"You gotta believe!" Waters kept crowing.

Starting at Dallas's 25-yard-line, with 1:46 left and no timeouts, Staubach hit pass after pass. A blitz-beating lob to Tony Hill and the extra-point kick put the Cowboys back in front, 35-34, with 39 seconds left.

The Redskins got in position to try a 59-yard field goal. But they weren't actually able to try it. Time ran out before the ball was snapped, securing one of the wildest games in a rivalry known for wild games.

Staubach notched his 14th comeback win in the last two minutes of regulation or overtime. He also racked up a slew of statistical feats: second-best passing yards in a game, club-record passing yards in a season, and another club record for touchdown passes in a season.

Just as the Cowboys suddenly had a lot to celebrate, the Redskins found themselves with a lot to stew over.

Washington would seemingly fall no farther than the second wild-card spot. The way the tiebreakers fell that season, the only way the Redskins would fall out of the playoffs was if they lost to the Cowboys and the Bears won their finale by at least 33 points. Well, Chicago—which hadn't won by more than 28 points all season—stuffed St. Louis, 42-6.

As everyone in the Redskins' locker room tried absorbing that news, Martin opened the door and flung in the wreath.

"They might as well take it home with them," Martin said. "They are the ones that need it. They are dead."

A few days later, Martin apologized in a telegram to Pardee. But, as Waters said, you gotta believe this is a game that'll never be forgotten by anyone involved.

7 Clint Longley was a shaggy-haired, rattlesnake-hunting slinger who led Abilene Christian University to an NAIA title in 1973, then left college after his junior year in an era when players rarely did that. The Bengals drafted him in 1974, then traded him to the Cowboys, who needed a third-stringer behind Staubach and Craig Morton.

When Dallas traded Morton to the Giants that October, Longley moved up to second string. He made his NFL debut six weeks later, jogging onto the field at Texas Stadium after Staubach was knocked out with the Cowboys trailing the Redskins, 16-3.

"I was afraid they weren't going to send me in," Longley joked that day. "But I was all they had left."

Only a few plays in, Longley threw a 35-yard touchdown pass to Billy Joe DuPree. His next series produced another touchdown, putting Dallas ahead, 17-16. Longley began to feel so comfortable in the huddle that he told veteran running back Walt Garrison to shut up.

The Redskins went back ahead, 23-17, and the game seemed likely to finish that way as the Cowboys took over on their own 40-yard-line with 1:45 left and no timeouts.

Longley kept hope alive by hitting Bob Hayes for six yards on a fourth-and-6. That helped, but they were still at midfield with 35 seconds left.

On second down, "The Mad Bomber" heaved one deep for Drew Pearson. Their 50-yard connection remains among the most electrifying regular-season plays in franchise history. Pearson slipped past defenders and hauled in the bomb around the 4-yard line, stepping into the end zone untouched.

The victory also prompted an all-time great quote, as offensive lineman Blaine Nye said this about Longley's performance: "This game represents the triumph of the uncluttered mind."

By '76, Longley was tired of being a backup—and the arrival of Danny White left Longley fearing where he'd land on the depth chart. His anxiousness began to boil one day on the practice field when he cursed at Pearson. The receiver didn't hear it, but Staubach did and stood up for his buddy. The two quarterbacks went out of the view of coaches to settle the matter.

While Staubach was a God-fearing family man, that didn't mean he was a wimp. Quite the opposite—he was a combat-trained military man. Longley was quickly reminded of that.

"Roger slammed him to the ground," Pearson said. "All of a sudden, Clint's feet were headed north and his head was facing south."

A few days later, Staubach was hooking together his shoulder pads in the dressing room when Longley sucker-punched him. The blow sent Staubach into a set of scales, opening a gash over his left eye. It took nine stitches to close and left a scar that's still visible. It also punched Longley's ticket out of Dallas.

He knew it, too, getting a young radio reporter to give him a ride to the airport in exchange for an interview.

Longley was soon traded to San Diego for a package of draft picks that would help Dallas land Tony Dorsett.

Longley spent a single season in San Diego, backing up another future Hall of Famer, Dan Fouts. Longley was cut in training camp the following year and never played in the NFL again. He played in the Canadian Football League and the short-lived World Football League.

Longley could've leveraged his Thanksgiving Day moment of fame into the occasional payday or at least some good fodder for "where are they now?" stories. Instead, he turned into a recluse, becoming the subject of several stories focused on trying to unlock the mystery of a mind that may have been more cluttered than Nye thought.

8 On Friday—yes, *FRIDAY*—September 30, 1960, in the second-ever game in franchise history, the Cowboys played host to the Philadelphia Eagles. Dallas lost, 27-25, launching what would become the most frequently played series in team history.

With the Eagles and Cowboys being division rivals for all but the very first season of Dallas's existence, their twice-a-year regular-season battles number 110. (They met once in 1960 and once in 1982, when the strike shortened the season.) The teams have also met four times in the postseason for an overall total of 114.

Some numbers:

- Dallas leads the regular-season series, 61-49.
- Dallas leads the postseason series, 3-1.

Since the postseason is what gives this rivalry its most-played status, let's take a look at those games.

The Eagles won Round I of this postseason series, and it was a biggie: the NFC Championship game after the 1980 season. Three weeks after Dallas beat Philadelphia at Texas Stadium, they met again at Veterans Stadium, where the Eagles had won the first meeting. This was Danny White's chance to lead the Cowboys to the Super Bowl in his first season after taking over for Roger Staubach, but Dallas mustered only 206 yards in a 20-7 loss that sent the Eagles to their first Super Bowl.

They met again in the first round of the playoffs following the 1992 season. Troy Aikman, Emmitt Smith, and Michael Irvin powered the way to a 34-10 victory that stands out because it put the Cowboys on the road to the first Super Bowl title of the Triplets era. In the 1995 postseason, Dallas again dumped Philadelphia in a first-round game on the way to the final Super Bowl championship of the Triplets era. The score was almost the same: 30-11.

The most recent playoff matchup came following the 2009 season. This game—a 34-14 Dallas victory—was the first playoff win in the careers of both Tony Romo and Wade Phillips, and it ended a franchise-worst, 14-year gap between playoff wins. Oddly, it was the second time in seven days that the teams played at AT&T Stadium. (The Cowboys had shut out the Eagles, 24-0, in the regular-season finale.)

Now let's talk about some memorable regular-season games. The common thread is one you might expect from a fan base that's best known for booing Santa Claus.

We'll start in 1987, in the first game following the players' strike, the one best remembered for the league's trying to bust the union by continuing to play games using replacement players—or "scabs." During that awkward time, Dallas used six regulars along with their replacement players to beat the Eagles, 41-22. Two weeks later, with both clubs back to full strength, they met again in Philadelphia. With the Eagles leading, 30-20, in the final minute, Randall Cunningham took a knee on consecutive plays. The seemingly routine kneel-downs were part of Philadelphia coach Buddy Ryan's evil master plan. On the next play, a third down from the 33-yard line with 11 seconds left, Cunningham faked another kneel, only to pop up and hoist the ball to Mike Quick in the end zone. A pass interference penalty moved the Eagles to the 1-yard line, and Ryan wasn't about to stop pouring it on. Philadelphia ran it in from there.

"I've been dreaming about that since we left Dallas," Ryan said.

Said Landry: "I wouldn't even justify that with a comment. Everybody has his opinion of what it was."

(Historic note: Future Cowboys coach Wade Phillips was on Ryan's staff that day. He was as disgusted as anyone. A few days before coaching in Philadelphia for the first time as head coach of the Cowboys, Phillips said that that episode caused him to be "the most embarrassed I've been in football.")

Another memorable game in the series came in 1989, just two years after the fake kneel-down. Ryan was still coaching the Eagles, but Jimmy Johnson had replaced Landry.

During a 27-0 rout by Philadelphia on Thanksgiving, Ryan allegedly offered his players a $500 bounty for taking out Troy Aikman and $200 for a hit that KO'd kicker Luis Zendejas. Zendejas, who'd been with the Eagles earlier that season, indeed went out with a concussion. Two weeks later, a rematch in Philadelphia was dubbed "Bounty Bowl II." The commissioner showed up to try to keep the peace. The Eagles won again, 20-10, and everyone left in one piece.

In 1999, the Cowboys were loaded up for one last run with the Triplets and went to the Vet having started the season 3-0. They were leading, 10-0, when Irvin caught a pass and went down hard on a turf widely considered the hardest and worst in the NFL. It turned out to be the final play of his career. And the fans cheered his motionless body.

This list could go on and on, but it has to end somewhere. So let's end on a high note—the signature moment of Jason Witten's career.

On a Sunday night in 2007, Witten caught a pass across the middle and was immediately smacked into by two Eagles defenders. The collision pried off Witten's helmet and sent both defenders tumbling to the ground. Witten stayed on his feet and took off running. The helmetless Witten didn't reach the end zone, but he did gain 53 yards and the respect and admiration of everyone watching. (In 2010, the NFL changed the rules so that a play is dead once a player loses his helmet.)

9 You can almost imagine Clint Murchison Jr. smiling over the fact that his favorite punching bag—the Washington Redskins—is the answer to this question.

Like the Eagles, the Redskins have been the Cowboys' division rivals for all but the inaugural season, which adds up to 110 regular-season matchups. The teams have met just twice in the playoffs.

Again, let's start with some raw numbers:

- Dallas leads the regular-season series, 66-42-2.
- Washington leads the postseason series, 2-0.
- Dallas has scored 2,532 points against Washington, its most against any team.

Since the rivalry between Murchison and George Preston Marshall already has been explored, this is a good time to review the next great clash of personalities in this series: Tom Landry vs. George Allen.

As coach of the Los Angeles Rams from 1966 to 1970, Allen got under Landry's skin by allegedly spying on Dallas practices. Did he really send people to watch their secret workouts? Or did he just want everyone to think he did? There's evidence both ways. Some facts are clear, though: Allen's Rams went 2-0 against Landry's Cowboys over the course of those four years, and in 1968, the NFL implemented anti-spying rules.

While Landry and Allen both specialized in defense, that was about all they had in common. Landry was calm and avoided personal relationships with players; Allen was volatile and often spoke publicly about which players deserved a raise.

Allen moved to the nation's capital in 1971, taking over the Redskins like a new political party moving into the White House. He replaced a slew of incumbents with his loyalists. In addition to bringing in guys from the Rams, he traded a pile of

A lighthearted moment between Tom Landry and his coaching nemesis, George Allen (right). (AP Photo/Charles Tasnadi)

draft picks for veterans. There wasn't a single rookie on the roster that season, underscoring his message, "The future is now." (Said Redskins president Edward Bennett Williams: "His father gave him a 6-week-old puppy when he was 4 and he traded it away for two 12-year-old cats.")

Allen's Redskins and Landry's Cowboys were 2-0 in 1971 games when they met for the first time. During the week leading up to that game, word got out about Allen having given a tryout to a quarterback named Steve Goepel. This was interesting, because Goepel had been drafted by the Cowboys and went to training camp with the team. It was also incredibly transparent. Remember, Allen made it clear he had no interest in having any youngsters on his team. Would he really make an exception for another team's discarded 12th-round pick? It appeared the real reason Allen brought him in was for a debriefing about Dallas's signals, tendencies, and any other information he could squeeze out of the kid. Allen halfheartedly dismissed those claims. Sensing that Allen was up to his old tricks, Landry moved midweek practice from the team's training facility to the Cotton Bowl just to be safe. Washington won the matchup, 20-16.

Landry and the Cowboys wound up going 8-7 against the Allen-coached Redskins. Yet Washington won the most important meeting: the rivalry's first-ever playoff matchup, in the NFC Championship game following the 1972 season.

Dallas was the reigning Super Bowl champs. But Washington and its "Over The Hill Gang" had won the division, ending the Cowboys' six-year streak of division titles. The Redskins stomped to a 26-3 victory to clinch their first trip to the Super Bowl.

The Allen-Landry hijinks continued. The Cowboys always rented out the hotel rooms that overlooked their own practice field whenever they played the Redskins to prevent giving Allen's confederates a bird's-eye view. Allen pulled stunts like turning off the hot water in the visiting locker room when Dallas played at RFK Stadium and bringing a giant cake into the locker room to celebrate a victory over Dallas in 1975. He also talked openly about his players wiping out Staubach.

"You never knew what he was going to do, what he was going to say," Landry once said. "He was always there spitting on his hands. That was George. He was good for the game, but we never trusted him."

Landry's final high-stakes game against the Redskins came after the 1982 season, when the more gentlemanly Joe Gibbs was leading Washington. Once again, a trip to the Super Bowl was on the line. Again, the Redskins won, this time leaving Danny White a game away from the big stage for the third straight year. He got knocked out of the game early and would never get that close again.

Among the memorable regular-season meetings was the 1988 victory in Washington, which proved to be the final win of Landry's career. There was no way of knowing it at the time, but it was emotional anyway, with center Tom Rafferty presenting Landry with the game ball in the locker room. "This is for a guy who stood by us, a guy who has taken a lot (criticism)," Rafferty said as teammates chanted, "T-L! T-L!"

Landry's rivalry with Washington was the backdrop of a classic American Express commercial from 1986. Set in the old West, Landry plays a cowboy. The premise is that you need to carry an American Express card, because, as Landry says, "you never know when you're going to be surrounded . . . by Redskins." To get the full effect, call it up on YouTube. While you're there, check out Landry crooning a knock-off of a classic Willie Nelson song in a commercial for a chain of discount hotels. Wearing his usual dapper sideline attire—including, of course, a fedora hat—Landry pops out of a suitcase, strums a guitar, and sings, "Mamas, don't let your babies grow up to be . . . Redskins."

One more aside to this rivalry belongs to Joe Theismann, the Washington quarterback whom Dallas fans loved to hate and who loved to be hated by Dallas fans. This bizarre relationship began during his playing days and continued during his years as a broadcaster. Snapshots of this rivalry within the rivalry include the 1978 game in Washington, when he ran around in the end zone, taking a safety while running out the clock in a 9-5 victory and then showing off the football to the defeated Dallas players; and the 1985 game at Texas Stadium, when the Cowboys intercepted him four times on his 36th birthday and fans serenaded him with a sarcastic rendition of "Happy Birthday."

In the Jerry Jones era, the juice of this rivalry returned to the ownership level when Daniel Snyder bought the Redskins. Jones and Snyder have been friends and enemies, battling and partying. Both are fans-turned-outsider-ish-owners who spend big, talk big, and dream big.

When Snyder hired Steve Spurrier to coach the Redskins in 2002, Spurrier announced that he looked forward to giving Snyder the game ball when Washington beat Dallas. He indeed did that following the season finale. However, let's end this section on a higher note—as in, what happened the first time those teams met that season.

Although the Cowboys were in the throes of an ugly time (three straight 5-11 seasons under Dave Campo), they also carried a nine-game winning streak over the Redskins into a Thanksgiving Day game. Emmitt Smith—who left the University of Florida when Spurrier took over as the head coach, turning pro at least in part because the incoming coach had no interest in his sticking around—had the last great game of his career. Smith, who was always at his best when motivated by a grudge, ran for 144 yards in a 27-20 victory. It would be the last victory in Dallas for both him and Campo, and it gave the Cowboys 10 straight wins over the Redskins, maxing out the longest winning streak for either team in series history.

(Note: This list skips games already described in previous answers. Keen observers may realize another satisfying Dallas victory is missing. It's coming later.)

10 Here's one you probably weren't expecting: the Rams.

The Cowboys and the Los Angeles Rams hooked up eight times from 1973 to 1985, splitting the series with four wins apiece.

It didn't matter where they played, either. Both teams won twice at home and twice in Los Angeles.

Seeing as George Allen was gone from the Rams by the time this postseason series began, it wasn't really a heated rivalry. Just two good teams whose paths kept crossing.

In the first meeting, a division-round game following the 1973 season, Los Angeles threw an interception on its first series and lost a fumble the next time it had the ball. The Cowboys used those turnovers to grab a 17-0 lead. But in the fourth quarter, Dallas's lead was down to 17-16. Deep in his own territory, Roger Staubach threw a pass to rookie Drew Pearson, who was just across midfield but also surrounded by two Rams defenders. Pearson caught the pass in stride and went to the end zone untouched on the way to a 27-16 victory.

Dallas's next two playoff wins over Los Angeles were biggies, because each sent the Cowboys to the Super Bowl. They also were biggies in the sense that the scores were lopsided.

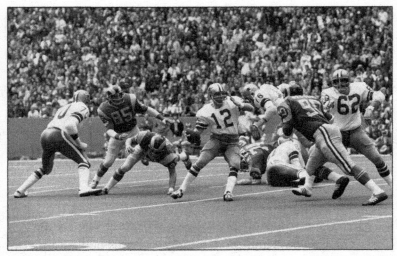

The Rams were a difficult playoff obstacle for Roger Staubach and the Cowboys. (AP Photo)

The Cowboys got to the NFC Championship game following the 1975 season thanks to the "Hail Mary" against Minnesota. Perhaps the Rams—who found themselves in the delightful position of hosting this game, rather than playing outdoors in Minnesota—were a little too comfortable and confident, as the Cowboys romped to a 37-7 victory. The surprise star was Preston Pearson, who caught three touchdown passes. Dallas became the first wild-card team to reach the Super Bowl, but Pittsburgh kept them from becoming the first wild-card team to win it all. (Since this is a trivia book, you should know that the first wild-card team to win it all was the 1980 Oakland Raiders. They beat a Philadelphia team that got there by ousting Dallas in the NFC Championship game.)

In 1978, the Cowboys and Rams met again for the NFC title. After a scoreless first half, Tony Dorsett put Dallas ahead with a 5-yard touchdown run. The Cowboys added three more touchdowns, capped by Thomas "Hollywood" Henderson's returning an interception 68 yards and dunking the ball over the crossbar in celebration. With the 28-0 victory, the Cowboys got their first chance to defend a Super Bowl title, only to be denied again by the Steelers.

Dallas's final victory in this postseason series came in Danny White's first-ever playoff start. The Cowboys racked up 528 yards on their way to a 34-13 victory in a wild-card game. The Rams may have once again been a little overconfident. Not only were they working toward a second straight trip to the Super Bowl, but also they were only two weeks removed from a 38-14 stomping of the Cowboys. If you're curious whether Dallas was motivated by revenge, here's what Tom Landry said after that playoff win: "Did you ever hear of the Alamo? You don't forget things like that."

11 Maybe knowing that Dallas has five postseason victories over San Francisco—its most against anyone—can help ease the sting Cowboys fans feel over the two infamous postseason losses to the 49ers.

The first two games were both NFC Championship games, and the victories sent Dallas to its first two Super Bowls. They also featured an interesting subplot: Tom Landry coaching against one of his protégés, Dick Nolan.

Nolan was Landry's teammate on the New York Giants, then Nolan played for Landry in New York and Dallas. Upon retiring, Nolan joined Landry's staff and was part of designing and implementing the Flex defense. After Dallas went to back-to-back NFL Championship games after the 1966 and '67 seasons, the 49ers hired Nolan to revive a team that had only a single winning season the previous six years. He had them a game away from the Super Bowl by his third season, only to have his old friends from Dallas get in the way.

The Cowboys beat the 49ers, 17-10, in the NFC Championship game following the 1970 season, then stopped the 49ers again, 14-3, the next year. They met for a third straight postseason, albeit this time in a division-round game. Dallas won again, 30-28, in a game remembered for one of Roger Staubach's classic comebacks.

Staubach had been out since October with a separated shoulder, but with Craig Morton struggling and the Cowboys trailing, 28-13, going into the fourth quarter, Landry figured he had nothing to lose and sent in No. 12. Calvin Hill got the rally started with a 48-yard run that set up a field goal, then Staubach did his thing, throwing a touchdown pass to Billy Parks with 1:20 left. Dallas recovered an onside kick, and then Staubach threw the game-winning touchdown pass to Ron Sellers. In that single quarter, Staubach went 12 of 20 for 174 yards and two touchdowns. Landry called it "the best comeback we've had since I've been in Dallas."

Their next postseason meeting was the NFC Championship game following the 1981 season, the game remembered by all football fans for Dwight Clark's making "The Catch" on what likely was a throwaway pass by Joe Montana.

Then came some classic matchups in the early 1990s.

The NFC Championship game following the 1992 season was played in Candlestick Park. It featured the Cowboys and their NFL-best defense against league MVP Steve Young and the 49ers' NFL-best offense. Dallas led, 24-20, in the final minutes, when Troy Aikman hit Alvin Harper on a short pass that turned into a long gain of 70 yards, setting up the victory-sealing touchdown. In the wild postgame scene, during the euphoria of having gone from 1-15 to Super Bowl-bound in a four-year span, Jimmy Johnson closed his celebratory speech by declaring, "How 'bout them Cowboys?!"

The juggernauts met again for the NFC Championship following the next season, only this time at Texas Stadium. Johnson ratcheted up the pressure on his team by having a few beers, then calling a local radio station and declaring: "We will win the ballgame. And you can put it in 3-inch headlines: We will win the ballgame!" Aikman helped Dallas build a 21-point lead before getting knocked loopy with a concussion. The Cowboys held on for a 38-21 victory—their fifth postseason win over the 49ers, fourth in NFC Championship games—and another trip to the Super Bowl.

Amazingly, the teams met in yet another NFC Championship game the next year. A turnover-filled start gave San Francisco a quick 21-0 lead, but Dallas battled back to get within 38-28. The Cowboys might've gotten even closer had officials flagged then-49ers cornerback Deion Sanders for interfering with Michael Irvin on a pass near the end zone, but it didn't happen. Dallas missed its chance for a third straight Super Bowl . . . and a sixth postseason victory over San Francisco. To Aikman, Emmitt Smith, and Irvin, this will forever be considered the one that got away.

12 It's those dang Eagles again.

Their 49 regular-season wins against Dallas are easily the most of any foe. And when you add that lone postseason victory, Philadelphia's tally hits an even 50.

Here's another record in Philly's favor, one that only makes sense considering the Eagles are the winningest foe:

They've also scored more points against Dallas than anyone else (2,187 going into the 2016 season; Washington is second at 2,113).

While we've already broken down many classic games of the Cowboys-Eagles rivalry, this opportunity begs for a few more, with the focus on games won by Philadelphia. So, Dallas fans, strap your chinstrap on tight, because the rest of this answer is going to be a bumpy ride down memory lane.

In 1991, the Cowboys went from being one of the league's most wretched teams to being a team on the rise. They sure didn't look like it during an early game against the Eagles, when they were stomped, 24-0, and fell to 1-2. The Triplets-led offense mustered a total of 90 yards that day and didn't cross midfield until the final minutes. Aikman got sacked 11 times, a record for both teams. He also threw three interceptions and lost a fumble. He had just 12 completions—including one to himself; Reggie White swatted a pass, and Aikman caught it for a loss of six yards. (It was the second and final catch of Aikman's career; the other was a 13-yard loss as a rookie.) Philadelphia's win was its eighth straight over Dallas, marking the longest-ever winning streak by any opponent.

"It was not a good day for anybody," Aikman said.

Another groaner came in the 2000 opener, the first game of Dave Campo's tenure as head coach. In retrospect, it fore-shadowed the Campo era. Philadelphia opened the game with a successful onside kick. Aikman's first five passes failed to hit their targets; then he went out with a concussion. Later, Joey Galloway suffered a season-ending knee injury. (Jerry Jones had traded two first-round picks to Seattle and signed Galloway to a $42 million, seven-year contract to give Aikman the deep threat that Jones believed was the final piece needed for another championship run. Aikman never completed a single pass to Galloway.) The final score of this game was 41-14, matching Dallas's worst margin of defeat in an opener. This game was also played in scorching conditions on the turf of Texas Stadium: kickoff temperature of 109 degrees, with on-field thermometers reaching upward of 130 degrees. The Eagles seemed to remain fresh, or at least more so than the Cowboys. Their secret weapon? Pickle juice. The salty water was supposedly a better elixir than traditional sideline beverages because it replenishes sodium levels faster, thus staving off muscle cramps.

On a Monday night in 2004, Donovan McNabb made the kind of play you have to see to believe. (Seriously. This description will try to do it justice, but do yourself a favor and call it up on YouTube.) It was third-and-10 from the Philadelphia 25-yard line, with the Eagles already up by 14 late in the first half. McNabb dropped back to pass, and Dallas lineman Leonardo Carson bolted through the middle of the line, right at McNabb. It looked like Carson was going to wrap him up, but McNabb spun to his right. Carson got a handful of the back of McNabb's jersey but couldn't hang on. McNabb then scrambled all the way back to the 8-yard line. Dallas's Greg Ellis was right in front of McNabb, so McNabb decided to see what he could find on the other side of the field. After nearly slipping, McNabb kept eluding Cowboys and nearly found his way back to the line of scrimmages, when he finally heaved the ball deep toward the middle of the field. The pass flew 54 yards in the air, hitting Freddie Mitchell in stride for a 60-yard gain and a play for the ages. The most incredible stat is that McNabb scrambled for 14.1 seconds.

Then, there's the 2008 finale, when the Cowboys flew to Philadelphia knowing that a win would put them into the playoffs for a second straight year. It was a chance to pick up the pieces from a rocky season and show that they were building something under Wade Phillips. Instead, they showed just how out of control things were, getting blown out 44-6 in a game that was even more lopsided than the score indicates. (And that score was the most lopsided Philadelphia victory in this series.) Tony Romo, who lost two fumbles and threw an interception, tried to be a good leader by holding an extended postgame news conference, yet even that backfired, as he ended up uttering one of the most-regretted lines of his career: "If this is the worst thing that ever happens to me, then I'll have lived a pretty good life."

13 The Steelers took out the Cowboys in two Super Bowls. The 49ers painfully kept the Cowboys from two Super Bowls. But neither team is the answer.

Nor is it Packers, who clipped the Cowboys in the play-in games to the first two Super Bowls and delivered the excruciating loss following the 2014 season; nor is it the Vikings, who knocked the Cowboys out of the postseason following the 1973, 1999, and 2009 seasons.

It's those Rams again, with four victories.

After losing its first two playoff games against Dallas, Los Angeles broke through in a division-round game following the 1976 season. Although the Cowboys were reigning NFC champions, they weren't really poised to get back to the Super Bowl because of a sorry running game (hence, the trade to acquire Tony Dorsett the following year). This was a weird game, one that saw Charlie Waters block two Rams punts and featured a pair of controversial calls that went against Dallas. The first was a 1-yard touchdown run by Lawrence McCutcheon that Landry claimed should've been ruled down outside the goal line, and then a fourth-down catch by Billy Joe DuPree that was ruled down just shy of a first down. The Rams won, 14-12.

Perhaps the most memorable game in this postseason series came in the division round following the 1979 season.

The Cowboys beat the Rams, 30-6, in the regular season and may have taken for granted that they would win again.

Vince Ferragamo threw a pair of touchdown passes in the second quarter to put the Rams up, 14-5, at halftime. Although Roger Staubach rallied Dallas to go ahead, 19-14, Ferragamo threw another touchdown pass with 2:06 left for a 21-19 lead. That left Staubach one last chance to get into field-goal range. On third-and-10 from the 33, Staubach wanted to throw to Ron Springs, but he was covered. Rather than risk taking a sack, Staubach tried to throw the ball away, but not so wildly that he'd get called for intentional grounding. He wound up drilling it into the belly of his left guard, Herb Scott. Because he was an ineligible receiver, that cost Dallas 10 yards. So now it's fourth-and-20. Staubach went deep to his favorite target, Drew Pearson . . . but a little too deep.

So there you have it: the final pass of Staubach's career was overthrowing Pearson, and his final connection was to Scott.

"Herb made a heck of a catch," Staubach said, laughing.

Another memorable part of this game is that Jack Youngblood snapped his fibula—the bone from the knee to the ankle—when hit by two players at once during the second quarter. He went to the locker room, got an X-ray, demanded tape and aspirin, and then went back in to face future Hall of Famer Rayfield Wright. Youngblood, himself a future Hall of Famer, somehow managed to get around Wright to sack Staubach. Youngblood kept playing on the broken leg in the NFC Championship game, the Super Bowl, and even the Pro Bowl.

Los Angeles's third postseason victory over Dallas came in a wild-card game in 1983. Although the Cowboys went 12-4 in the regular season, they'd stumbled into the playoffs with lopsided losses to Washington and San Francisco. Dallas continued stumbling in the postseason, blowing a third-quarter lead by turning the ball over on four straight series: a fumbled punt and three interceptions by Danny White. Los Angeles won, 24-17.

As bad as that was, the '85 game was worse.

On a day when Rams quarterback Dieter Brock completed just six passes for 50 yards, the Cowboys were helpless against the Los Angeles offense because of the other guy in the backfield: Eric Dickerson. In a performance reminiscent of his great days at SMU, Dickerson romped for touchdowns of 40 and 55 yards on his way to a total of 248. It was the most ever against the Cowboys (regular season or postseason, topping the 232 Jim Brown once put up), the most ever by a Ram, and a record for an NFL playoff game. Dallas's offense was as dismal as its defense, never getting within 20 yards of the end zone. The final score was 20-0 in what turned out to be Tom Landry's final playoff game.

14 Harvey Robert "Bum" Bright made pro sports history in 1984 when he bought the Dallas Cowboys for $60 million and spent another $20 million on the lease to Texas Stadium. It was the most money ever paid for a franchise.

In February 1989, Bright was again involved in the most lucrative deal involving a pro-sports franchise when he sold the Cowboys and the lease to Texas Stadium to Jerry Jones for $140 million.

So in five years, Bright turned $80 million into $140 million. For all the clutch plays and big wins by players and coaches celebrated in this book, Bright deserves recognition as one of the biggest winners. (Of course, Jones turns out to be the bigger winner, as his $140 million investment led to a franchise that *Forbes* says is worth $4 billion and is the flagship of a family empire.)

Bright was always a keen businessman. After serving in World War II, he returned home to Texas and began buying oil and gas leases. They turned him into a millionaire by age thirty-one, letting him expand his holdings to banking, real estate, and trucking.

Cowboys founder Clint Murchison Jr., meanwhile, was squandering his oil fortune through bad investments and bad behavior. He sold the team to try to keep his debtors at bay, but even the $80 million payday wasn't enough. He owed hundreds of millions of dollars when he died a few years later.

Bright cited both good business and civic duty as reasons for buying the team. (Truth be told, he was far more of a Texas A&M fan than a Cowboys booster.) Murchison attached two requests to the sale: Bright had to keep Tex Schramm and Tom Landry, and Bright had to follow Murchison's lead as a hands-off owner.

The team was already spiraling, and things would soon get worse. In the first season of Bright's signing everyone's paychecks, the Cowboys missed the playoffs for the first time in a decade, suffered their most losses in 19 years, and failed to have a starter in the Pro Bowl for the first time in 21 years.

Dallas made the playoffs the next year, only to suffer its first (and still only) postseason shutout. Tom Landry's streak of winning seasons ended the next year.

In 1988, First Republic Bank Corp. failed, costing Bright about $29 million in stock, and his other businesses were in trouble; so in August, he began looking into selling the Cowboys. Jones was on vacation in Mexico when he saw something about this in the *Wall Street Journal*. Still angry at himself for not hav-ing done more to purchase the club in '84, the Arkansas oil man could hardly believe that a second chance was coming his way.

While the financial transaction was going on, the Cow-boys stumbled to a 3-13 season. Finally, in February 1989, a deal was done—well, almost. There was one last matter to be resolved: $300,000 in closing costs.

Bright proposed letting a coin toss decide it. He even let Jones make the call. Jerry went with tails, and it landed on heads. Jones not only paid the closing costs, but he later received a framed two-headed coin from Bright with a note that read, "You'll never know."

Bright died in 2004. He was eighty-four.

15 OK, all you keen observers from answer No. 9 in this section. This is that other memorable Cowboys-Redskins game intentionally omitted so we could delve into it here.

It was November 5, 1989, and the Cowboys beat the Red-skins, 13-3, in a night game at RFK Stadium. Let's hit the highlights:

- The Redskins came in 4-4, and the Cowboys were 0-8. Washington was getting back its starting quarterback, Doug Williams. Dallas was without its leader, Troy Aikman.
- Steve Walsh replaced Aikman and wasn't very good. He completed 10-of-30 passes for 186 yards and took three sacks. He threw no touchdowns but at least avoided any interceptions.
- Williams, in his first game since back surgery, went 28-of-52 for 296 yards with two interceptions.
- Weeks after the Herschel Walker trade, the Cowboys' start-ing running back was Paul Palmer. He ran for 110 yards,

including a 47-yarder that would've been longer had he not run out of gas. Once he caught his breath, he plowed into the end zone from the 2 for the touchdown run that put Dallas up, 10-3, in the third quarter. He also had a 14-yard burst in the fourth quarter, setting up a 43-yard field goal by Roger Ruzek that sealed the victory. This was the only 100-yard game of Palmer's career.

- The Cowboys didn't have a single turnover or penalty. Their defense, which had been giving up 29 points per game, didn't even allow a touchdown. They also limited the Redskins to 50 yards rushing.

"The rocky days are not over for the Cowboys," Jimmy Johnson said. "But we're going to have a lot of wins over the next so many years in Dallas. It's just good to get started."

In addition to this being Dallas's first win of the season, it was only the second victory in 21 games. Both came against Washington in Washington, the other being the final victory of Landry's career. (Again, it's easy to picture Clint Murchison Jr. smiling over this.)

While we're on the subject of 1989, and since we've brought up Walsh, this is a good time to explore both.

You know by now all the tumult of the turnover of ownership, management, and coaching. You also know about the Walker trade.

But we haven't mentioned that the Cowboys went 3-1 in the preseason, with Johnson coaching those exhibition games as if he had something to prove. The only thing he accomplished was building false hope. He found this out the hard way in the opener, getting spanked, 28-0, by the New Orleans Saints. Dallas would get shut out twice more this season.

The Cowboys went 0-11 in games started by Aikman. Palmer led the team in rushing with a mere 446 yards. There are more gory details, as you'd expect from a team that goes 1-15.

One of the more curious aspects of the '89 season was the presence of Walsh.

When Johnson took over, he not only inherited the No. 1 overall pick, but he also had a slam-dunk, no-brainer selection in Troy Aikman—a ready-made franchise quarterback for a franchise in desperate need of a quarterback. Wanting either to hedge his sure-thing bet or to inspire competition, Johnson used a supplemental draft pick on Walsh, who'd led Johnson's Miami Hurricanes to a national title in 1987 and won 23 of their last 24 games together. By acquiring Walsh this way, Johnson had to give up the next season's first-round pick, which would've been No. 1 overall.

So, let's review: the newbie leaders of a rebuilding team spent a valuable future commodity to stir up trouble with perhaps their best future asset.

Walsh lacked the size and the arm of Aikman, but, hey, at least he knew how to make Johnson happy.

The quarterback controversy never really developed, and Walsh's presence became a mere footnote. And about that No. 1 overall pick Dallas squandered to get him? Well, Trader Jimmy ended up trading Walsh to New Orleans for first-, second-, and third-round picks, a decent return on an investment for a guy who'd never be more than a mediocre quarterback.

16 When Tom Landry created the 4-3 defense, he envisioned the middle linebacker as being the key—the quarterback of the defense. So he didn't offer that position to just anybody.

Landry invented the scheme when he was the defensive coordinator on the New York Giants, and Sam Huff was the first guy trusted with this job. Jerry Tubbs was the first great middle linebacker in Dallas. He even made the Pro Bowl in 1962, the year before the Cowboys spent a first-round pick on the next great middle linebacker: Lee Roy Jordan, the pride of Excel, Alabama.

Jordan's tenacity—and, some might say, nastiness—came from his hardscrabble upbringing. The fourth boy among seven kids, he grew up on a farm where the family raised animals and grew cotton, vegetables, and sugar cane. They turned the sugar cane into syrup, which they then traded for groceries. Football was young Lee Roy's ticket out, and it was punched by Paul "Bear" Bryant at the big school in his home state.

The Crimson Tide went undefeated and won its first national championship under Bryant during Jordan's junior year. The following season, Jordan was a unanimous All-American; in his final college game, he made 31 tackles to help shut out Oklahoma in the Orange Bowl.

"Lee Roy takes it mighty personal when anybody comes at him with a football," Bryant once said.

Because Tubbs was still going strong, Jordan broke in as an outside linebacker. He moved to the middle in 1966. That's also the year the Cowboys began their streak of 20 straight winning seasons.

At 6-foot-1, 220 pounds, Jordan was relatively small for his position. He compensated in several key ways. He took home game films to study long before that became a common practice. And then there was his legendary toughness, the attitude, and the quality that prompted teammates to refer to Jordan as "Killer."

"He'd hit his grandmother if she had a helmet on," running back Walt Garrison said. "Six days a week, I hated Lee Roy. But on Sundays, when he was on my side, I loved him like a brother."

As great a player as Bob Lilly was, he wasn't a vocal or emotional leader. Jordan kept waiting for someone like that to emerge before deciding he might as well do it himself. Case in point came during the third quarter of the NFC Championship game following the 1970 season, with the game tied and the San Francisco 49ers pinned close to their own end zone.

In the huddle, Jordan looked at each player and screamed, "Somebody's gonna make the big play! Somebody's gonna stop them!" This turned out to be the Cowboys' version of Babe Ruth calling his shot, as Jordan intercepted a pass at the 17-yard line. Duane Thomas ran into the end zone on the next play, giving Dallas a lead it wouldn't relinquish on the way to its first Super Bowl.

That's leadership. That's Lee Roy Jordan.

He finished his career with 154 consecutive starts and 1,236 tackles, the most in franchise history (since surpassed by Darren Woodson).

Despite his greatness from 1963 to 1976, Jordan had to wait until 1989 to get into the Ring of Honor. Of course, there's a story behind that.

A contract dispute in 1973 prompted Jordan to walk out for 24 hours, which in turn prompted Tex Schramm to call him a traitor. Schramm gave him a new contract, but he also

Lee Roy Jordan (55) could be a one-man wrecking machine, bulldozing his way to the most tackles in team history when he retired. (AP Photo)

vowed never to let him into the Ring of Honor. Righting this wrong was one of the first things Jerry Jones did when he took over as the sole decider of Ring membership; he made Jordan the first player enshrined in the Ring of Honor during his ownership, doing so in 1989.

17 Of all the characters in Cowboys history, Walt Garrison may be the most endearing.

How else do you describe a guy who, as a rookie, would sneak out of the team hotel the night before games to go enter bulldoggin' (steer-wrestling) events at the local rodeo? A guy who needed 36 yards of tape to prepare his body for a Super Bowl?

Garrison grew up in the Dallas suburb of Lewisville, a rapidly growing area now that in his day was so small that "There was one main street and the biggest deal that ever happened was when they paved that street."

Oklahoma State University was the only college that offered him a scholarship, and that was only because he knew someone who knew someone. (Once Garrison got to Stillwater, Oklahoma, the coach of his freshman team turned out to be Sammy Baugh.) Garrison parlayed his years as an OSU Cowboy into becoming a fifth-round pick of the Dallas Cowboys in 1966. (Garrison once asked Darrell Royal why the Texas Longhorns never tried to recruit him. "Well, Walt," Royal said, "we took a look at you and you weren't any good.")

Garrison became Dallas's starting fullback in 1969 and a mainstay in the lineup through 1974. His blocks helped pave the way for Calvin Hill to set club rushing records in 1972 and '73.

Asked once whether he considered lobbying for a raise, Garrison said, "If the Cowboys paid me what I was worth, I'd lose money."

During one training camp, Garrison picked up a hunk of wood and a knife and began whittling. The carvings became his go-to activity, and he became incredibly skilled at it. To this day, many of his amazing creations are on display at his ranch, known as "The House That Snuff Built," due to the fortune he made shilling for chewing tobacco.

He'll never be in the Ring of Honor, much less the Hall of Fame. But for as long as people talk about the Dallas Cowboys, they'll be telling tales about Walt Garrison.

18 Although Michael Irvin played for Jimmy Johnson in college and they enjoyed some glorious days together in Dallas, especially once Troy Aikman and Emmitt Smith arrived, the fact remains: Irvin was drafted by Tex Schramm, Tom Landry, and Gil Brandt.

After going 7-8 in the strike-shortened 1987 season, the Cowboys had the 11th pick in the 1988 draft. Linebacker Aundray Bruce went first overall to Atlanta. Tim Brown was the first receiver taken, going to Oakland at No. 6. Green Bay followed by taking another receiver, Sterling Sharpe. Once the New York Giants took guard Eric Moore with the 10th pick, Dallas was able to get its man.

Irvin grew up in Fort Lauderdale, Florida, the 15th of 17 children. That was a lot of mouths to feed, and there wasn't always enough of anything to go around, which sometimes led to young Michael getting in trouble. Walter Irvin got his son into a private Catholic high school in hopes of straightening out his life. The older Irvin died soon after, when Michael was seventeen, so he never saw his son become a star at that high school and beyond. Playing for Jimmy Johnson at the University of Miami, Irvin set school career records for catches, yards, and touchdowns and led the Hurricanes to an undefeated season and a national championship in his junior year. With nothing left to prove—and fame and fortune awaiting—he turned pro.

Perhaps Irvin's brash personality was the fresh blood this sagging franchise needed. Schramm thought so. In declaring that Irvin would help revive the Cowboys, Schramm symbolically connected the team's past and future by having Irvin wear Drew Pearson's old number—88, of course.

Irvin had a solid rookie season, catching 32 passes for 654 yards and five touchdowns. But that was with Steve Pelluer at quarterback. Everything changed early in 1989, when Jerry Jones and Johnson took over, and they spent their first draft pick on Troy Aikman. The connection Irvin and Aikman forged would land both of them in the Hall of Fame. And after Emmitt Smith joined them the next season, the Cowboys fulfilled Schramm's vision of reclaiming their spot atop the NFL.

Irvin led the league in receiving yards and yards per game in 1991, the year before this era's first Super Bowl season. He put up even better numbers in 1995, the year of Dallas's final championship. His career numbers could have been even better if not for his penchant for getting stopped around the 1-yard line, giving Smith so many short touchdown runs. (Fantasy football players from those days surely remember this.)

While stats were important to Irvin, winning trumped all. That desire, along with his trash-talking and work ethic— all of them legendary—made Irvin the heart and soul of the 1990s Cowboys. It's no coincidence that when his life began to unravel, so did their dominance.

In March 1996, police interrupted Irvin, who was celebrating his 30th birthday in a motel room with strippers and drugs, leading to a trial that ended with his pleading no contest to felony cocaine possession. At training camp in 1998, he reportedly brawled with teammate Everett McIver, gashing his neck with scissors—an incident that could've led to Irvin's parole being revoked had police gotten involved. (They didn't.) More drama followed, from legitimate issues to false accusations.

Forced to retire because of injuries, Irvin left the NFL with the ninth-most receiving yards in league history and tied for the ninth-most catches. His mega-watt smile, gift of gab, and knowledge of the game make him a regular on television.

Aikman, Smith, and Irvin, the trio by which all other collections of QB-RB-WR are judged. (AP Photo/Tim Sharp)

The Triplets went into the Ring of Honor together in 2005. Two years later, Irvin got his spot in the Hall of Fame. Before Irvin spoke, Jones introduced him with these words that so perfectly summed up his impact:

"In the locker room, he was a teammate first, a competitor second, and a superstar third. His leadership style not only transcended the cliques in the locker room, but his leadership style on our team and our organization went from the locker room and the equipment room all the way to the board room. It permeated it. I don't know that we'll see again a professional football player with a combination of his strength and his skills as an athlete on the field and his unbelievable people skills. Smart, resourceful, communication, charm, the kind of charisma and tremendous will with the strength to get the respect of the team. He had his faults. But in a unique way that only Michael Irvin could pull off."

19 Peter Gent was one of the greats at Michigan State, a dominant force who left his mark all over the school's record book—in basketball.

Football? He hadn't played that since high school. But the Cowboys were paying people just to try out, so he figured what the heck. Dallas liked his combination of athleticism and size (6-foot-4, 205 pounds), envisioning him as a receiver. Gent apparently liked the idea, too, as he chose the NFL over a shot at the NBA (though it was a long shot, as the Baltimore Bullets took him in the 14th round).

Gent spent five seasons on the Cowboys, starting sometimes but always in the rotation—first at receiver, then, after knee injuries slowed him, at tight end. He caught four touchdown passes and left a more lasting contribution in this advice given to a rookie seen concentrating deeply on his playbook: "Don't bother reading it, kid. Everybody gets killed in the end."

Gent was traded to the Giants after the 1968 season, a fitting time for him to leave considering his good buddy Don Meredith retired then, too. Gent never played a down for New York, yet he would be heard from again a few years later—as an author.

In the early 1970s, players didn't write tell-all books. So Gent cloaked his best stories in the novel *North Dallas Forty*, a book that became even more popular once it was made into a movie starring Nick Nolte and Mac Davis. (Gent helped write the screenplay.)

North Dallas Forty focuses on quarterback Seth Maxwell and his receiver pal, Phil Elliott. The team is called the North Dallas Bulls, coached by B.A. Strothers.

While the book depicts plenty of debauchery, it also explores the way the NFL chews up players and spits them out. The novel peeled back the curtain on pain and drugs being constants in the NFL, making it clear that the two are connected; players used painkillers to stay in the lineup, and alcohol and recreational drugs to dull their injuries and fears of getting cut.

The book drew many accolades, though not from the football establishment. Tex Schramm led the crusade against it, calling the book "a total lie."

"What has happened is one person, who in my opinion has a sick approach to life, has indicted the whole NFL and the Dallas Cowboys organization," Schramm told the *Washington Post* after the book came out in 1973.

Gent wrote several more books, including a memoir about raising his son. Gent died in 2011 at sixty-nine.

20 Unlike the arrival of Tony Dorsett and Emmitt Smith, the drafting of DeMarco Murray was quite unheralded.

Despite his record-setting career at Oklahoma—a school known for producing great running backs—Murray was the sixth running back taken in 2011, going to Dallas in the third round with the 71st overall pick.

Murray began his rookie season as the third-stringer behind Felix Jones and Tashard Choice. He had just 14 carries over his first four games. Then Jones sprained an ankle, and Murray got a chance to shine. He turned 11 carries into 34 yards that afternoon, but it was good enough to earn him the starting job the next week.

And that's when Murray showed he was something special.

Murray ran over the St. Louis Rams for 253 yards, which was more than Dorsett, Smith, or any other runner in Cowboys history gained in a single game; it was 10th-best in NFL history. The performance included a 91-yard touchdown run that was the second-longest in club history, behind only Dorsett's NFL-record 99-yarder.

DeMarco Murray blossomed into the most successful running back of the post-Emmitt era. (AP Photo/Sharon Ellman)

Murray led the club in rushing that season and each of the next three years. Only Smith (13 straight years), Dorsett (10), and Don Perkins (five) had longer streaks. Yet Murray also missed significant action in his second and third seasons because of injuries, reviving concerns about his durability—one of the knocks that dropped his draft stock.

Two thousand fourteen was his only full season as a starter. And, wow, what a season it was.

Murray ran for a franchise-record 1,845 yards. That was best in the NFL, as were his 13 rushing touchdowns, 392 carries, 115.3 yards per game, and 2,261 yards from scrimmage. He had 12 100-yard games, including a streak of eight in a row to open the season, breaking the record of six straight set by Jim Brown way back in 1958. He was named the NFL's Offensive Player of the Year. As for the knock on his durability, he debunked that by breaking his hand in the second-to-last game, having surgery the next day, and returning to rush for exactly 100 yards and a touchdown in the finale.

If anything, that season proved to be too good, as the Philadelphia Eagles lured Murray away with a contract bigger than what Dallas was willing to pay. Tony Romo and Jason Garrett lobbied hard to keep him, but Murray took the money and ran. (The Eagles offered a guaranteed $21 million; the Cowboys were only willing to guarantee him $12 million.) He proved to be a bad fit in Philly and after just one season was dealt to Tennessee.

21 Charles Haley and DeMarcus Ware are the Cowboys' most dominating pass rushers since the early incarnations of the Doomsday Defense. While they wore the same number and had similar skill sets, they couldn't have been more opposite as people.

Haley was such a loose cannon that the San Francisco 49ers gave up on him after he helped them win two Super Bowls. How difficult was he? After a loss to the Raiders during the 1991 season, Haley punched through a glass door. Ronnie Lott had to calm him down. This is significant, because Lott played for the Raiders at the time. Someone had to fetch Lott from the winning locker room and urge him to come help Haley.

During training camp before the 1992 season, the 49ers were so willing to get rid of a twenty-eight-year-old, two-time Pro Bowler that they swapped him for a second-round pick and a third-rounder. Crazier still, they dealt him to Dallas, an up-and-coming NFC team that seemed to be missing only a dominating pass rusher like Haley.

Jerry Jones himself picked up Haley at the airport. It was an olive branch extended to show how much the team valued him and the first step toward harnessing his anger. (After he retired, Haley was diagnosed as being bipolar.)

On the field, Haley lived up to expectations. With him anchoring the defensive line rotation, the Cowboys had a defense ready to complement its high-powered offense. In his first four seasons in Dallas, the Cowboys won three Super Bowls and were a win away from playing for another title.

In 1996, Haley's back problems limited him to five games, marking the beginning of the end of his career and of Dallas's demise.

Haley resumed his career—in San Francisco, of all places—but was never the same dominant force. Yet nobody can forget him at his peak. The fact that he's the only player with five Super Bowl rings guarantees that. So does his spot in the Ring of Honor and the Hall of Fame, which came in 2015.

In his induction speech, Haley credited his ex-wife for recognizing in 1988 that he had manic depression and blamed himself for not having dealt with it. He urged others not to make the same mistake. Haley was diagnosed with bipolar disorder several years after he retired.

"The only way that you can grow is that you've got to ask for help. . . . Today, guys, I take my medicine every day, and I try to inspire others to do the same, and that's because I finally listened," he said.

Ware arrived in Dallas as the 11th pick in the 2005 draft. There was some debate as to whether Bill Parcells and the front office would pick Ware or linebacker Shawne Merriman. It's pretty clear now that the Cowboys got this one right.

Parcells was changing Dallas to a 3-4 defense and needed a dominant pass rusher. He compared Ware's speed and playmaking ability to that of the greatest defensive player he ever coached, Hall of Fame linebacker Lawrence Taylor.

The only question about the soft-spoken, sweet-natured Ware was whether he might be too nice.

Yet Ware showed a nasty edge on the field by getting to quarterbacks early in his rookie season. His sack totals rose from 8 to 11.5 to 14 to a league-best 20 in 2008. That was the most by a Cowboy since sacks became an official statistic in 1982. (The unofficial team record for a season is 23, by Harvey Martin in 1977.) Ware led the league again in 2010, although with "only" 15.5. The next year, Ware nearly became the first player with a pair of 20-sack seasons, reaching 19.5.

After the 2013 season, the Cowboys made the painful decision to let Ware go. He was thirty-one, coming off a career-low 6 sacks, and, if he stayed, his contract would've taken up a huge chunk of the team's salary cap.

Over nine years with the Cowboys, Ware racked up 117 sacks, the most in franchise history. (Martin had 114, according to team records, as the sack didn't became an official stat until late in his career.)

"DeMarcus Ware, through his performance on the field and his outstanding character, is someone who is held in the highest regard within the Dallas Cowboys family," Jones said in a statement announcing Ware's release. "He is worthy of our greatest respect and we want what is best for him and his family."

Ware landed in Denver and went on to play a starring role in the Broncos' Super Bowl title following the 2015 season.

22 On December 4, 1960, the Dallas Cowboys pulled off a first in franchise history: they didn't lose.

In their first-ever game against the New York Giants, Eddie LeBaron brought the Cowboys back from deficits of 14-0 and 21-7. Despite a rib injury that almost kept him from starting, LeBaron threw three touchdown passes, capped by an 11-yarder to Billy Howton with 2:37 left to secure a 31-31 finish. The NFL didn't have overtime in the regular season until 1974, so that was as good as it got for the newbies in their expansion season. (Tidbit for the hard-core trivialist: technically, the tie was sealed by Fred Cone's point-after kick.)

The game was played at Yankee Stadium in front of 55,033 fans—the biggest crowd to see the Cowboys all season. Dallas had a bit of an advantage in that Tom Landry had spent the previous decade with the Giants, first as a player, then as a player-coach, then as the assistant coach in charge of the defense (what we'd now call the defensive coordinator, although back then there was just one assistant on each side of the ball). The fact that the Giants went from division champions in his last two seasons there to 6-4-2 also-rans in the first season without him indicates how vital of a contributor he'd been.

When the Cowboys returned to Dallas following this momentous near-breakthrough, fans were waiting at Love Field to celebrate this accomplishment.

Actually, it was just two people. And the commemoration was limited to a sign that read, "Well Done, Dallas."

23 The franchise's first victory came in the first game of the next season, on September 17, 1961, against the Pittsburgh Steelers.

Don Meredith started, but he and Eddie LeBaron pretty much took turns running the offense. LeBaron put the Cowboys ahead early with a 44-yard touchdown pass to Fred Clarke. In the third quarter, LeBaron threw a 45-yard touchdown pass to Billy Howton on a flea-flicker that put Dallas up, 17-14.

Bobby Layne marched Pittsburgh to a tying field goal. Then Meredith threw a touchdown pass to Johnny Sample— that is, defensive back Johnny Sample. His 39-yard interception return put the Steelers ahead, 24-17, with 5:52 left.

Meredith later delivered a 17-yard touchdown pass to Dick Bielski, tying the game with 56 seconds left. That was plenty of time for Layne to drive for the winning points, but Dallas linebacker Jerry Tubbs intercepted a pass at the Dallas 38 with 10 seconds left.

LeBaron threw to Howton for a 41-yard gain. The wise veteran made sure to go out of bounds, stopping the clock. (More on Howton: In 1963, while still playing for Dallas, he became the NFL's career leader in receptions with 503 and receiving yards with 8,459. To show how far the passing game has come since then, he ranked 75th in yards and 126th in receptions when the 2016 season began.)

Howton's move set up Allen Green for a 27-yard field goal. Despite the short distance, it was no gimme.

Playing his first NFL game, Green had already missed two field goals and had a punt blocked. But this one flew between the uprights, solidifying the milestone victory in glorious fashion.

24 In November 2006, when Tony Romo burst onto the scene and "Romo-mania" was at its peak, everything and anything about him made for a great story—even the tale of why he wore No. 9.

Romo was torn on whether to reveal it. So he turned it into a game, daring reporters to crack the code.

His first hint was that it came from a New York baseball team. The obvious guess is Roger Maris, the home run hero of the New York Yankees. But Romo eliminated anyone who played for the Yankees or Mets. It also wasn't anyone who played for the Brooklyn Dodgers or the New York Giants.

There's a Hollywood tie-in to the story of why Tony Romo wears No. 9. (AP Photo/LM Otero)

Clue No. 2 was even more cryptic: Buffalo's War Memorial Stadium.

Hmm. The Buffalo Bills played there from 1960 to 1972, as did baseball's Buffalo Bisons of the International League.

It also was where the movie *The Natural* was filmed. That's the flick featuring Robert Redford as an older-than-usual rookie sensation for the New York Knights. The character's name is Roy Hobbs, and he wore No. 9.

It's uncanny how their tales overlap.

After two-plus seasons of being nothing more than a holder, Romo got his big chance in October 2006 and seized it in a way that would seem implausible if it came from Hollywood. Consider:

- In his first start, he led the Cowboys to a franchise-record 25 fourth-quarter points.
- In his second start, Terrell Owens dropped what would've been a victory-sealing touchdown. Dallas only ended up losing because of a wacky sequence that let Washington kick the winning field goal after time had expired.
- Over the next three games, all victories, Romo was named NFC Player of the Week twice. In the game he wasn't honored for, Romo completed 19 of 23 passes as the Cowboys knocked off the reigning Super Bowl champion Colts, who were 9-0 at the time.

His fifth start was probably the most dazzling, as he tied a team record with five touchdown passes, before the third quarter even ended. And this came in his first Thanksgiving start. (Before the game, some fans strung up letters spelling out his name in the Ring of Honor, at least until security made them take it down. After the game, a well-lubricated Jerry Jones joked that he was going to fire those security guards.)

Hobbs, er, Romo continued his charmed life off the field. He dated starlet Jessica Simpson, then country singer Carrie Underwood. He judged the Miss Universe pageant and landed all sorts of endorsement deals. While he's yet to live up to the hope and hype generated by those first few months, there's no denying that he brought the Cowboys much-needed stability at quarterback for an entire decade.

Back in the locker room in those heady days in 2006, Romo was asked if he had that star quality known as "it."

"I don't know what 'it' is," Romo said. "You try and work hard and get better each week. I play the game with passion. I enjoy the game. It's a lot of fun when I'm out there. That's the way I play. For some reason, people like that."

25 Even with all the disappointment of the last 20-plus years without a Super Bowl appearance, the Cowboys are still known for their championship pedigree. So it may be hard for modern-day fans to recognize that the Cowboys were once known as choke artists.

You know the type: always a bridesmaid, never a bride. Can't win the big one.

Or, as sportswriter Steve Perkins dubbed them in the title of his book about the 1968 season, the Dallas Cowboys were "Next Year's Champions."

You've already read about the near-misses in 1966 and '67. Well, the Cowboys were so poised for greatness in '68 that Perkins kept a diary of sorts and turned it into a book. The team wound up getting bounced in the division round of the playoffs in '68 . . . and '69. They were oh-so-close to being great yet couldn't get over the hump. (Yep, there's another cliché that fit.)

They finally reached the Super Bowl in 1970—and blew it in the final minute. Instead of shaking their reputation, the Cowboys enhanced it. It's worth noting that Landry's reputation was equally tarnished; he wasn't being hailed as a football genius, like he is now, but rather as the guy who wasn't getting the most out of his talent.

A year later, the breakthrough came. The Cowboys won it all, and Landry was carried off wearing a smile of relief so wide that Roger Staubach talked about it at the coach's memorial service. By the time the label of "America's Team" was applied, Dallas had long since distanced itself from its close-but-no-cigar ways.

26 Everson Walls made the greatest play of his career long after his retirement.

From his perspective, he was just looking out for his best friend.

Walls and Ron Springs became teammates and fast friends at training camp in 1981. Springs was in his third season and about to become the starting fullback in front of Tony Dorsett; Walls was an undrafted rookie who would not just make the roster, but lead the league in interceptions.

Yet Walls's rookie season is most remembered for a play he failed to make. You may be familiar with it; folks often refer to it as "The Catch."

Yep, Walls is the unfortunate No. 24 reaching in vain as Dwight Clark snatches the pass that Joe Montana may or may not have been trying to fling out the back of the end zone, giving the San Francisco 49ers the winning touchdown in the NFC Championship game following the 1981 season.

Walls actually had two interceptions in that game, and it's quite possible the Cowboys don't even get to that game without his league-leading 11 interceptions that year. (Note: no NFL player has had more than 10 interceptions in a season since.)

Walls led the league in interceptions again the next year and yet again in 1985. His 44 career thefts are second-most in team history, behind only the 52 by Hall of Famer Mel Renfro.

Walls left after getting into a tiff with Jimmy Johnson in 1989. He resurfaced with the New York Giants, arriving just in time to help them win the Super Bowl and getting the ring Clark may have prevented him from earning nearly a decade before. Sweeter still, Walls and the Giants advanced to that Super Bowl by winning the NFC Championship game in San Francisco.

Springs, meanwhile, played with the Cowboys through 1984, then spent two seasons in Tampa Bay.

The friendship between Walls and Springs endured no matter what happened in their professional careers. They became the godfather to one of each other's children, and their wives became best friends. They took family vacations together. Springs even spoke at the funeral for Walls's father-in-law.

Springs was only thirty-four when he was diagnosed with diabetes. In 2004, at age forty-seven, he began having kidney problems. They caused him so many circulation problems that doctors amputated his right foot and two toes on his left foot, while his hands became balled into knots. He endured dialysis three times a week. Springs needed a new kidney but refused to accept one from his children—including his son, Shawn, who was then playing for the Washington Redskins—because he feared his kids would become diabetic and would need both their kidneys. Walls discovered he was a match, so he gave Springs one of his kidneys.

The transplant occurred early in 2007, making Walls the first professional athlete known to have donated an organ to a teammate. Later that year, Springs underwent a far more minor procedure to have a cyst removed from his forearm. Complications left him in a coma. Springs died in 2011. He was fifty-four.

The two started a charity to educate people about chronic kidney disease and about being a donor. It's called the Gift For Life Foundation. Walls later wrote a book titled *A Gift for Ron: Friendship and Sacrifice On and Off the Gridiron.*

27 Chad Hennings fulfilled two of the most popular dreams that kids have.

Become a fighter pilot? Check.

Win a Super Bowl? Check, check, check.

Hennings flew 45 missions during the first Gulf War. For those keen on military trivia, he flew A-10s, the only jets capable of accommodating his 6-foot-6, 290-pound frame.

He arrived in Dallas at only twenty-six, but five years removed from playing football. He showed up the same year as Charles Haley. And while Hennings didn't have the impact Haley did, Hennings still played a crucial role as part of the posse in a defensive line rotation that kept pass-rushers fresh without giving the opposing offense much of a rest.

Hennings became a starter at right defensive tackle in 1995 and held that job until his body wore out in 2000.

He started 72 of his 119 career games and piled up 27.5 sacks and 216 tackles. Those aren't Ring of Honor-type stats, but there is a "what might've been" component to it. After all, he was such a star player at the Air Force Academy that in 2006 he was inducted into the College Football Hall of Fame.

Considering all his leadership training, it's no surprise that teammates chose him as their union representative when that job came open.

His amazing personal narrative makes him a natural as a motivational speaker. He's also written three books.

Hennings carries two other nifty claims: He and Roger Staubach are the only players in franchise history to have attended a service academy and served in the military before joining the club; and the way things turned out, he flew a fighter jet *and* won a Super Bowl in the same year.

Success in the military and in the NFL. Hennings truly enjoyed the best of both worlds.

28 First, an admission: this was basically a trick question.

Only two of the Cowboys' eight head coaches were NFL head coaches before being hired in Dallas: Bill Parcells and Wade Phillips. If you decoded that part of the answer to realize this was an either-or question, then you probably went with the guy who won two Super Bowls and is in the Pro Football Hall of Fame.

Still, let's look at the numbers:

COACH	PREVIOUS TEAMS	PRE-DALLAS RECORD
Bill Parcells	Giants, Patriots, Jets	138-100-1
Wade Phillips	Saints, Broncos, Bills, Falcons	48-42

Parcells's arrival is a fascinating turning point in franchise history.

The 2002 season had just ended, and the Cowboys were about as low as could be. Not only were they coming off three straight 5-11 seasons, but Jones was widely perceived as an overbearing boss. Since splitting with Jimmy Johnson over credit for back-to-back Super Bowl titles, Jones had hired and fired Barry Switzer, Chan Gailey, and Dave Campo—three straight coaches widely viewed as "puppets." The roster wasn't too attractive, either.

It was the very fact that the Cowboys were in such shambles that intrigued Parcells.

Realizing how little leverage Jones had, and how badly he needed someone credible, Parcells cut himself a sweet deal. While he wouldn't get free reign to "pick the groceries," as he'd so famously demanded during his Patriots days, he'd sure get a lot of input.

From the minute he arrived, Parcells commanded more respect than Campo ever had. Players trusted there was a method to his madness, even when he devoted much of his first training camp to working on situational plays. (True story: the very first drill of his very first training camp practice required quarterbacks to throw deep balls *out of bounds*.)

Dallas lost its first game under Parcells, then went to the Meadowlands in a nationally televised return to the site of his greatest glory. Facing the New York Giants on a Monday night, the Cowboys let a 15-point lead turn into a three-point deficit with 11 seconds left.

Then the situational work paid off.

Rookie Zuriel Smith knew to let a wayward kickoff roll out of bounds. Quincy Carter connected on a pass designed to set up a last-second field goal. Billy Cundiff kicked a 52-yarder to force overtime, and then Carter set up Cundiff for the game-winner.

Anyone in the Cowboys locker room who didn't already consider Parcells a coaching genius surely deferred to him now.

The Cowboys went on to win five straight—remember, they won five games *total* each of the previous three years—and finished the season 10-6, the best they would do in Parcells's four-year tenure. Dallas even went to the playoffs that season, only to get wiped out by Carolina.

You know what else happened in 2003? Arlington taxpayers voted to build the team a new stadium. It's fair to question whether that happens without Jones repairing his image by hiring Parcells and, more important, Parcells having such an immediate impact.

The Cowboys failed to make many moves the next offseason, sliding to 6-10. A pair of 9-7 records followed, but Parcells's final season also marked the start of the Tony Romo era.

Parcells went 34-30 in Dallas, plus 0-2 in the postseason. He had more success at each of his other stops (reaching at least the conference championship), but there's no doubt that his time with the franchise was transformational. Simply put, the Cowboys were a lot better off when he left than they were when he arrived.

29 Not as tricky as the previous question, but still one that becomes kind of easy once you decode it.

Tom Landry, Barry Switzer, Dave Campo, and Bill Parcells never coached anywhere after Dallas. Jason Garrett was entrenched going into the 2016 season. So that brings the pool of candidates down to three guys: Jimmy Johnson, Chan Gailey, and Wade Phillips.

The answer, as you may have already realized, can be written in three-inch headlines.

COACH	FUTURE TEAMS	POST-DALLAS RECORD
Jimmy Johnson	Dolphins	36-28
Chan Gailey	Bills	16-32
Wade Phillips	Texans*	0-3

Phillips was defensive coordinator and took over as head coach after Gary Kubiak was fired.

After his high-profile divorce from the Cowboys, Johnson dabbled in television for two years. Then Don Shula retired, and the former University of Miami coach replaced him, giving Johnson the incredible distinction of following the coaches who were Nos. 1 (Shula) and 3 (Landry) on the all-time NFL wins list.

For one of the rare times in his coaching career, Johnson was mediocre with the Dolphins. His teams went 8-8, 9-7, 10-6, 9-7, reaching the playoffs three times but never winning more than a single game each postseason. He actually resigned after the third season, only to return a day later when Dan Marino asked him to give it one more try. Johnson walked away for good after the following year, going out with a humiliating 62-7 playoff loss to Jacksonville and then returning to the good life of watching and talking about games on Fox's studio show.

A native of Port Arthur, Texas, Johnson grew up going to school with folk star Janis Joplin, then went to the University of Arkansas. Jerry Jones was a teammate and Barry Switzer was one of the assistant coaches.

Johnson got into coaching right out of college, working his way up to defensive line coach at Oklahoma, then defensive coordinator at Arkansas. He went to Pitt as defensive coordinator and assistant head coach and got his first head coaching job at Oklahoma State in 1979. He went to Miami in 1984 and built a college football dynasty.

The Super Bowl in January 1989 was played at Joe Robbie Stadium in Miami. Tex Schramm invited Johnson to join himself, Gil Brandt, and Tom Landry at their box for the big game. Dallas would eventually need someone to replace Landry, so it only made sense for them to get to know this native Texan who was winning big in college.

About a month later, Jones bought the Cowboys, fired Landry, and hired Johnson. Much of this book has detailed the incredible series of events that followed as they stripped the team down to 1-15 and built it up to Super Bowl champions in 1992 and '93. Then the simmering tensions between the JJs turned into an inferno. Johnson agreed to leave and got a hefty check as a going-away gift.

It remains to be seen whether Jones ever puts Johnson in the Ring of Honor. Odds are it never happens. But it sure is fun to imagine a silhouette of his helmet hair on that prestigious wall, à la the fedora next to Landry's name.

30 The turnaround under Jimmy Johnson hit its stride in 1991. A pivotal game was the Sunday before Thanksgiving, when the Cowboys were trying to bounce out of a 1-3 funk against a Washington team that was 11-0.

Dallas led 14-7 when Aikman went down with a knee injury on the final play of the first half. Steve Beuerlein took over in the third quarter, and the Cowboys didn't miss a beat.

They won that game, 24-21. They won the next four games, as well. That made them 11-5, locking up a wild-card berth into the playoffs.

Beuerlein's roll continued as he guided the Cowboys past the Chicago Bears, setting up a division-round game against the Detroit Lions. Aikman was healthy now, but Beuerlein got the nod.

He also ended up getting the hook after throwing an interception that was returned 41 yards for a touchdown, putting Dallas behind, 14-3.

Aikman did OK in his first-ever playoff appearance, but not enough to lead the Cowboys to a victory.

His first postseason start came in 1992. Aikman would win his first seven postseason starts and 11 of his first 12.

As for Beuerlein, the long winning streak on his watch was more of an indication of the talent this team had beyond its starting quarterback. From halftime of the Redskins game until he got pulled from the Lions game, Beuerlein completed 81-of-163 passes—less than 50 percent. He never threw more than one touchdown pass in a game but, for the most part, avoided interceptions.

To borrow a phrase from Bill Parcells, Beuerlein was a bus driver. But in 1991, he kept the Cowboys' brewing dynasty on time for arrival the next season.

THIRD QUARTER

ALL-PRO LEVEL

Now we're really kicking things up a notch. After all, every team has 22 starters. But only the very best across the entire league can earn the distinction of being an All-Pro. Are you up to the challenge?

1 The Dallas Cowboys have been to a whopping eight Super Bowls, winning five and losing three. This is about the sites of those games. *Answer on page 135.*
   • What city has hosted the most Super Bowls featuring the Cowboys?
   • In what city have the Cowboys hoisted the Lombardi Trophy the most often?

2 The Cowboys have been to the top of the NFL—winning the Super Bowl—more often they've been at the very top of the NFL draft. Still, they have made the No. 1 overall selection on a handful of occasions. *Answer on page 136.*
   • How many times?
   • Can you name the years and the players they took?

3 Bill Parcells's overhaul of the Cowboys began with the 2003 draft. He took Jason Witten in the third round and snagged Tony Romo as an undrafted free agent. *Answer on page 138.*
   • Name the other two members of that draft class who started more than 100 games for the Cowboys.

- Bonus: The only other relatively accomplished player to emerge from that class was a center who played 48 games for Dallas, starting 31. Name him.

4 Throwing a touchdown in a postseason game is always memorable. It's even more memorable when passing isn't your primary job. Only twice in franchise history has a nonquarterback pulled off this feat. *Answer on page 140.*

- In the Ice Bowl, halfback _____ hurled a 50-yard touchdown pass.
- In the Super Bowl following the 1977 season, fullback _____ threw a 29-yard touchdown pass.
- Bonus: Name the receivers who caught those passes.

5 While it seems like the Cowboys have always played on Thanksgiving Day, that hasn't always been the case. What year did the tradition begin? (Bonus if you know the origin story.) *Answer on page 142.*

6 Who scored the first Super Bowl touchdown in team history? *Answer on page 144.*

7 Who am I? *Answer on page 145.*
- In the first round of the 1998 draft, the Cowboys selected me instead of Randy Moss.
- Late in my career, I became known for grousing about my contract, my role . . . or both.
- After reluctantly moving from defensive end to linebacker, I tore my Achilles tendon. The next year, I recorded the most sacks of my career, earning my first (and only) trip to the Pro Bowl and getting named the NFL Comeback Player of the Year.

8 Nineteen seventy-nine was the final season of Roger Staubach's career. During the draft earlier that year, the Cowboys

could've spent the 76th pick on Joe Montana. Instead, they took tight end _____, letting Montana go to the San Francisco 49ers at No. 82. *Answer on page 146.*

9 In the Cowboys' first Super Bowl victory, Roger Staubach threw touchdown passes to two future Pro Football Hall of Famers. Name them. *Answer on page 147.*

10 In the early 1970s, the Cowboys embarked on an overseas version of their Kicking Karavan. Who proved to be their prized discovery? *Answer on page 149.*

11 Going into the 1992 playoffs, Jimmy Johnson knew the Cowboys were on the cusp of greatness, so he wasn't about to ease up. He decided to make an example out of a player by cutting him following a sloppy performance in the meaningless season finale. Name the player he used as a scapegoat. As a bonus, what was his sin? *Answer on page 151.*

12 Perhaps the most infamous decision Barry Switzer made as coach of the Cowboys was running a play called _____ on fourth down in the closing minutes of a tie game in Philadelphia while on *his own* 29-yardline. It failed, but the 2-minute warning went off, giving Switzer a chance to change his mind. (Bonus: what did Switzer call on the do-over?) *Answer on page 152.*

13 The Cowboys have held their preseason training camps all over the country. Their journey has included six states, hitting multiple cities within some of those states. How many sites can you name? *Answer on page 154.*

14 It only makes sense that the Cowboys and the Houston Oilers regularly squared off in the preseason. Yet back

in the 1960s, it took the settlement of a court case to launch this in-state matchup. Who was the player at the center of the disagreement? *Answer on page 157.*

15 When Troy Aikman was knocked out of the NFC Championship game following the 1993 season, backup _____ replaced him, holding down the fort in the second half against the San Francisco 49ers to send the reigning Super Bowl champion Cowboys back to defend their title. *Answer on page 159.*

16 During his holdout prior to the 1971 season, running back Duane Thomas held a news conference during which he ripped Tom Landry, Tex Schramm, and Gil Brandt. What memorable labels did he pin on them? (Bonus: what was Schramm's classic retort?) *Answer on page 161.*

17 Who am I? *Answer on page 163.*
- In college, I was a two-time All-American player—in basketball. I didn't play football in college.
- I was so out of my element that I needed help putting on my pads. But I figured out how to play cornerback well enough to make the All-Rookie team.
- I went on to make five Pro Bowls, three times at cornerback and twice at safety. I started in two Super Bowls, winning one. When my playing days ended, I became a scout for the Cowboys and later the Broncos.

18 Tex Schramm loved occasionally taking wild swings in the draft. For instance, in 1967, he spent an 11th-round pick on Pat Riley—yes, *that* Pat Riley. In 1985, Schramm spent a fifth-round pick on USFL star Herschel Walker just to own his rights in case the rival league folded.

What obscure choice did Schramm make in the 12th round of the 1984 draft? (Hint: this athlete would begin carving his legacy in another sport just a few months later, never giving football a thought.) *Answer on page 164.*

19 The Dallas Cowboys Cheerleaders became a sensation when they debuted in 1972. But the club actually had a squad of cheerleaders before them. Who were they? *Answer on page 165.*

20 In 2009, Michael Irvin hosted a reality TV show to find an NFL player, with the winner getting invited to the Dallas Cowboys training camp. Name the winner, who indeed made the team. Bonus points for naming the show. *Answer on page 165.*

ALL-PRO LEVEL – ANSWERS

1 Let's take a look, game by game:

GAME	SITE	RESULT
Super Bowl V	Orange Bowl, Miami	Lost to Colts, 16-13
Super Bowl VI	Tulane Stadium, New Orleans	Beat Dolphins, 24-3
Super Bowl X	Orange Bowl, Miami	Lost to Steelers, 21-17
Super Bowl XII	Superdome, New Orleans	Beat Broncos, 27-10
Super Bowl XIII	Orange Bowl, Miami	Lost to Steelers, 35-31
Super Bowl XXVII	Rose Bowl, Pasadena, California	Beat Bills, 52-17
Super Bowl XXVIII	Georgia Dome, Atlanta	Beat Bills, 30-13
Super Bowl XXX	Sun Devil Stadium, Tempe, Arizona	Beat Steelers, 27-17

So Miami's Orange Bowl is the Cowboys' most frequent Super Bowl home—and their most tortured. All three of Tom Landry's Super Bowl losses came there, all by less than a touchdown.

New Orleans is the only city where the Cowboys have won multiple titles, and they happen to be the first two in franchise history. Note the use of the word *city*, as those championships were claimed at different stadiums.

The first big game in the Big Easy was held at Tulane Stadium. The temperature at kickoff was 39 degrees, still the coldest in Super Bowl history. Dallas's defense froze Miami's offense—holding the Dolphins without a touchdown, still the only time that's happened in a Super Bowl—on the way to the franchise's first championship.

When the Super Bowl returned to New Orleans, the elements were no issue, because the game was played inside the climate-controlled Louisiana Superdome. It was the first indoor Super Bowl, and the Cowboys had no trouble with either the elements or the Denver Broncos.

It's noteworthy that the five Super Bowls of the Landry era were held in just two cities, while the three Super Bowls of the Jerry Jones era were spread to three sites.

2 In 1974, using a pick acquired from the Houston Oilers, Dallas took defensive end Ed "Too Tall" Jones from Tennessee State University.

In 1989, using a pick earned by going 3-13 the previous season, Dallas took quarterback Troy Aikman from UCLA.

In 1991, using a pick acquired from the New England Patriots, Dallas took defensive tackle Russell Maryland from Miami.

And that's it. Across 56 drafts, the Cowboys have used the No. 1 overall pick a mere three times.

Dallas also earned the first overall pick in 1990 by going 1-15 in 1989 but forfeited it in advance by having used a supplemental draft pick on quarterback Steve Walsh of Miami in 1989.

(Note: The Cowboys have picked second overall twice, both with picks acquired via trade. These are notable because of who they got: Randy White in 1975 and Tony Dorsett in '78. Both wound up in the Hall of Fame, coincidentally going in together in 1994. Dallas was also supposed to have the No. 2

pick in 1961 but had traded it to Washington in the deal for quarterback Eddie LeBaron.)

Let's use hindsight to review each of Dallas's No. 1 picks.

Jones played a franchise-record 224 games, stretching from Bob Lilly's final season to Troy Aikman's first. He started in three Super Bowls, made three Pro Bowls, and led the team in sacks three times. And that was with Jones taking off the 1979 season to dabble in boxing. (He went 6-0, with five knockouts.)

Was Jones the best possible choice? Well, the '74 draft produced five other guys who made the Hall of Fame: Pittsburgh standouts Mike Webster, Jack Lambert, Lynn Swann, and John Stallworth; and Oakland's Dave Casper. There's no telling how those guys would've done in Dallas, and with Too Tall's sustained success, you can make a strong case that he was a worthy pick.

Aikman's feats are all over this book, most notably leading the Cowboys to three Super Bowls in four years. While the '89 draft also included Hall of Famers Barry Sanders, Deion Sanders, and Derrick Thomas, there's no doubt Aikman was the right choice.

Maryland's selection came with an asterisk pretty much from the start. He was a consolation prize. The Cowboys had traded up to No. 1 to get Raghib "Rocket" Ismail, but he spurned the NFL to sign with the Toronto Argonauts of the Canadian Football League. (Ismail eventually came to the NFL and, from 1999 to 2001, was a solid player for the Cowboys, catching passes from Aikman just like Jerry Jones dreamed he would in 1991.)

Maryland spent five seasons in Dallas and was a nice cog on the defensive line rotation during the Super Bowl run of the 1990s. He even made a Pro Bowl. However, retrospect shows a lot of other guys who might've fit in nicely. But the Cowboys don't have to feel too badly. Every team had a chance to get the best player to emerge from that draft—Brett Favre—as he lasted until the 33rd pick.

3 When Bill Parcells was working for ESPN and thinking about getting back into coaching, he could've taken practically any opening. And if he was looking for a fixer-upper, he had plenty to choose from.

But to put it in Parcells-like terms, when you remodel a broken-down trailer home, all you end up with is a really nice trailer home; when you remodel a dilapidated mansion, you end up with something special.

So the challenge of rebuilding "America's Team"—and the added challenge of doing it under Jerry Jones—appealed to him.

Step 1 of his plan: conquer the draft.

While his best pick came in the third round (Witten with No. 69 overall) and the Romo signing was a post-draft move, Parcells found a few more solid contributors.

Cornerback Terence Newman never lived up to his status as a fifth overall pick, but he was a very good player for nine years. He intercepted 32 passes over 131 starts and made the Pro Bowl twice.

Linebacker Bradie James was a great pick for a fourth-rounder.

After first grabbing attention on special teams, James became a starter in 2005. He started every game for six straight seasons, leading the Cowboys in tackles every season. That six-year streak as the top tackler matched the longest in team history. James had more than 100 tackles in each of those seasons, including a whopping 202 in 2008. He finished his Dallas tenure with 1,009 tackles, sixth on the team's career list. He also was a vocal leader, serving as a defensive captain from 2006 to 2010.

Linebacker Bradie James was a long-lasting value pick from Bill Parcells's first draft with the Cowboys. (AP Photo/Ross D. Franklin)

In May 2014, after one season in Houston, James announced his retirement—as a Cowboy. He signed a ceremonial one-day contract and savored a final chance to speak to a gathering of reporters. (Fittingly for this answer, the media was assembled at Valley Ranch for a pre-draft news conference.) Sitting next to James, Jerry Jones called him "a player that gave it everything he had."

So if Newman was the first-rounder, Witten the third-rounder, and James the fourth-rounder, then a good bet for the bonus answer is the second-rounder.

His name is Al Johnson, and he was a center taken from Wisconsin. Instead of taking over as the starter, as expected, he underwent microfracture surgery on his right knee before his rookie season even began. He returned to make his debut in 2004, playing every game and starting 15. He started every game the next year, too, then lost his spot to Andre Gurode. Johnson later played one season for Arizona and one more in Miami.

For the record, the Cowboys made three other picks in 2003: defensive back B.J. Tucker and receiver Zuriel Smith in the sixth round, and guard Justin Bates in the seventh. Tucker played in ten games, Smith in nine, and Bates never made the club. (You may recall Smith from answer 28 in the Starter section.)

4 Long before Dan Reeves made a name for himself as a head coach in the NFL, he proved himself as a jack-of-all-trades on the Cowboys.

He could run. He could block. He could catch passes. He held for field goals and extra points. He returned a few punts and kickoffs and, one time, even kicked an extra point. When his playing days were fading, he took on the unique role of player-coach.

Reeves could also throw. He'd been a quarterback in college at South Carolina, although not a very distinguished one. He completed 48 percent of his passes for the Gamecocks and wasn't drafted. Still, from 1965 to 1972—the entire span of his playing days in Dallas—Reeves threw at least two passes every season. He threw only one in his postseason career, but it was a doozie.

It came in the NFL Championship game following the 1967 season, a.k.a the Ice Bowl. The Cowboys were trailing the Green Bay Packers, 14-10, in the fourth quarter. Since little else was working, Reeves and Don Meredith decided to see whether Reeves might have any luck throwing the ball from midfield.

After a poor first half, Reeves had since run six times for 40 yards. This is important, because it helped sell the play.

Seeing Reeves take a handoff, the Packers figured it was just another sweep, so the cornerback and safety came up to stop him. When Reeves pulled up and looked deep, he saw Lance Rentzel wide open. He also heard beaten cornerback Bob Jeter swear at him.

All Reeves had to do was get the ball somewhere near Rentzel. Throwing a heavy ball through the wind, he came close enough. Rentzel turned to have his entire body facing the line of scrimmage to make sure he hauled in the pass at the 20-yard line. He trotted into the end zone with a touchdown that gave Dallas its first lead of the game, 17-14, with about five minutes left.

Had Bart Starr not scored on a quarterback sneak in the closing seconds, the Reeves-to-Rentzel 50-yard pass probably would be hailed as one of the top plays in franchise history.

As for Robert Newhouse, he had no extensive experience at quarterback.

Newhouse threw two passes in 1975, completing one, both on gimmick plays. In the weeks leading up to the Super Bowl following the 1977 season, Tom Landry decided to try it again. They practiced it often, but it never worked.

That's why everyone in the huddle was so surprised when he called it during the Super Bowl.

The Cowboys were already ahead, 20-10. The way their defense was playing, the Broncos were lucky to be that close. Dallas had just recovered a fumble 29 yards from the end zone with about seven minutes left when Landry decided to try the trick play.

"I was shocked," Newhouse said.

He was also concerned—not because of what he was being asked to do, but because his throwing hand was coated with

"Stickum," a glue-like substance players used to make it easier to hold and catch the ball. The stickiness is counterproductive when trying to throw, so Preston Pearson handed Newhouse a towel. He rubbed off as much as he could and nibbled at the rest.

Roger Staubach took the snap and tossed it to Newhouse, who was moving to his left. He took about 10 steps, pulled up, and heaved the ball toward the end zone. Golden Richards had two defenders with him, but the ball floated over them—narrowly avoiding a swat by Broncos cornerback Steve Foley—and into the receiver's hands for the championship-sealing touchdown. It also made Newhouse the first running back ever to throw a touchdown in the Super Bowl.

Newhouse died in 2014. He was sixty-four.

5 In 1863, President Abraham Lincoln declared that the final Thursday in November would always be celebrated as Thanksgiving.

In 1892, William Heffelfinger became the first player known to be paid to play football.

In 1920, pro football was played on Thanksgiving for the first time.

And in 1966, the Dallas Cowboys got in on the fun.

Here's how those final pieces fell into place.

The Detroit Lions became regular Thanksgiving hosts in 1934. Starting in 1953, they had the only pro game that day. When the rival AFL began in 1960, they, too, celebrated the holiday by playing a single game. In 1966, NFL commissioner Pete Rozelle wanted to up the ante with a second game and needed a team to host it. His old friend Tex Schramm volunteered.

Other clubs were hesitant, because they feared that their fans would consider a home game on Thanksgiving an imposition on their family time. Schramm, however, was a University of Texas alum and knew the annual Thanksgiving game between the Longhorns and the Aggies had a huge following. Why not give it a try at the NFL level?

The debut came on November 24, 1966, almost exactly three years after Dallas became known as the city where President John F. Kennedy was assassinated, and the Cowboys faced the Cleveland Browns. The game drew a club-record 80,259 fans to the Cotton Bowl, plus another team first: the game was televised in color. Everyone liked what they saw as Don Meredith led the Cowboys past the Browns, 26-14.

Quick side note on those Browns: Cleveland was among Dallas's first rivals. The Cowboys came into the NFL in the Browns' division, so they met twice a year. With Jim Brown in the backfield and Paul Brown on the sideline, Cleveland won 11 of the first 12 meetings. Once Dallas blossomed into a competitive team, Jim and Paul Brown were gone, and the Cowboys won four straight. Cleveland got the last laugh, though, knocking Dallas out of the playoffs following the 1968 and '69 seasons before switching to the AFC.

Back to Thanksgiving, though. Dallas became such a fixture that other teams began whining about it. They said the Cowboys always had an unfair advantage by getting 10 days off before their next game (ignoring the fact that they had only four days to prepare following the previous game and forgetting that this "advantage" hadn't exactly turned the Lions into a powerhouse).

In 1975 and '77, the league took the Thanksgiving games away from the Cowboys, letting the St. Louis Cardinals play host instead. TV ratings plummeted, so the networks made sure the NFL rectified the situation. Dallas went into the 2016 season owning a record of 29-18-1 on Thanksgiving.

In 1997, the Cowboys' reputation was flagging because of a series of off-field incidents. Jerry Jones's daughter, Charlotte Anderson, came up with an idea to do something positive: a halftime concert during the Thanksgiving game featuring a big-time act, with the network airing the whole thing and including a charity tie-in. Since Thanksgiving is the traditional kickoff of the Salvation Army's red-kettle campaign, spotlighting them made perfect sense. Two decades later, the mid-game performance has become a regular part of the holiday tradition.

6 It was first-and-goal from the 7-yard line with 8:16 left in the second quarter of Super Bowl V. Dallas and Baltimore were tied at 6 when Craig Morton took the snap, faked a handoff to his left, dropped back a few more steps, and threw a screen pass to his right.

Duane Thomas caught the ball around the 13-yard line and went around a block by tight end Pettis Norman. Inside the 5, Colts safety Jerry Logan got low to try upending Thomas, but the running back moved sideways just enough to bounce off a blow from Logan's shoulder pads. One step later, Thomas was wrapped up from behind by the arms and body of defensive tackle Billy Ray Smith. However, both players' momentum was going forward, and they tumbled together into the end zone, which was painted blue with the word *Colts* in white.

Thomas got up, handed the ball to the official, and trotted off with a nice slice of team lore: its first-ever Super Bowl touchdown. Officially, it came on a 7-yard pass.

Note: Dallas's first points in a Super Bowl came from the right foot of Mike Clark, who booted a 14-yard field goal with 5:57 left in the first quarter to put Dallas ahead, 3-0. He also kicked a 30-yarder in the second quarter to stretch the lead to 6-0 before Thomas's touchdown made it 13-6.

7 Greg Ellis did all he could to be known as more than The Guy Dallas Took Instead of Randy Moss.

Yet even after Ellis's very solid 12-year career, we can't help but open a review of his career without a wistful reflection on what might've been.

The Cowboys went 6-10 and missed the playoffs in 1997. Just two years after their run of Super Bowl titles ended, the franchise was clearly going the wrong way. The offense needed a young playmaker, and the big, strong, fast Moss seemed like the perfect solution.

Problem was, the franchise was dealing with all sorts of off-field turmoil, headlined by Michael Irvin's motel drug bust and trial. And Moss carried a lot of baggage. This proved to be one of the few instances where Jerry Jones gave in and took the safe route. You could argue that one of the reasons it became so rare has to do with how this decision backfired.

Again, Ellis was a nice, solid player; but Moss was a special talent, as he would show the Cowboys on Thanksgiving of his rookie season. Moss—who said he wanted to make the Cowboys pay for not drafting him—caught just three passes, all for touchdowns: a 51-yarder followed by a pair of 56-yarders. He finished the season with a league-leading 17 touchdowns.

Moss played seven career games against Dallas, eight if you add in a playoff game. His team won them all. He caught a total of 40 passes for 789 yards (that's 19.7 yards per catch) with 11 touchdowns.

Now, about Ellis . . .

He started at defensive end the first eight years of his career, averaging 6.5 sacks per season. He was also a good guy in the locker room, getting voted both team captain and the team's representative to the players' union. (That's significant, because character is what swayed Dallas from Moss. And while Moss had a few highly publicized incidents, he wasn't the kind of law-breaker the Cowboys feared.)

When Bill Parcells decided to switch from a 4-3 defense to a 3-4, he wanted Ellis to become a linebacker. Ellis did so grudgingly. Then he tore his Achilles tendon. As he fought to return, Dallas spent a first-round pick on Anthony Spencer, who was essentially a younger version of Ellis. Fearing that he was being phased out, Ellis wanted a new contract. He got it and responded with his best season: a career-high 12.5 sacks in just 13 games, as he missed the first three while still recovering.

Ellis lasted one more season in Dallas before he was released. He played one season with the Raiders before calling it a career.

Over 11 seasons with Dallas, Ellis had 77 sacks; only DeMarcus Ware (117) and Jim Jeffcoat (94.5) had more since sacks became an official stat.

8 The Cowboys went into the 1979 draft with Roger Staubach secure as the starter, Danny White being groomed as his replacement, and Glenn Carano coming off the first year of his apprenticeship.

So when it was Dallas's turn to pick in the third round of that draft and the best player available according to their ranking system was another quarterback, a debate ensued. Tom Landry brought up the possibility that the Cowboys would cut the rookie at the end of training camp, because they didn't have a roster spot for another quarterback.

We'll never know what Joe Montana might've done in Dallas. But we do know what he did for the 49ers and against the Cowboys, specifically in the NFC Championship game following the 1981 season.

We also know what happened with the guy the Cowboys took instead—Doug Cosbie.

Cosbie spent 10 seasons in Dallas, working his way up from Billy Joe DuPree's backup to the starter in 1982. Cosbie made the Pro Bowl following the 1983, '84, and '85 seasons. What made him unique was that he was a pass-catching tight end in an era when the position was still mostly manned by blockers.

In 1984, he caught 60 passes for 789 yards and four touchdowns, setting club records for catches and receiving yards by a tight end. He broke both marks the next year when he caught 64 passes for 793 yards and six touchdowns. He retired with 300 receptions for 3,728 yards and 30 touchdowns. (He began to realize the end of his career was near when an opposing coach asked him what his plans were after football. That coach? Bill Parcells, then of the Giants.)

While Cosbie and Montana will always be linked, there's an interesting twist to the story: on the day their paths most famously crossed, Cosbie nearly became the guy who made the big play.

With 10:41 left in the fourth quarter of that NFC Championship game, Cosbie caught a 21-yard touchdown pass that put Dallas ahead 27-21. It could've been the play that got White and the Cowboys to the Super Bowl, if not for the Montana-to-Dwight Clark play known as "The Catch."

Cosbie, by the way, grew up in the Bay Area (Palo Alto, specifically) and attended Santa Clara University. He returned to his old stomping grounds after leaving the Cowboys, first serving as an assistant coach at his alma mater and then spending two years as an assistant coach at Stanford . . . working under Bill Walsh.

9 Mike Ditka and Lance Alworth were among the aging stars brought in to help get the Cowboys their first championship.

Alworth was thirty-one, Ditka thirty-two. In 1971, Alworth was in his first season in Dallas, Ditka his third. Both would play one more year before retiring.

Neither had a particularly standout regular season. Alworth caught 34 passes for 487 yards and two touchdowns (worst since his rookie year), and Ditka had 30 catches for 360 yards and one touchdown. Then again, the Cowboys struggled on offense much of the year as Landry struggled to choose between Staubach and Craig Morton at quarterback. The offense was also at its best when the ball was in the hands of running backs Duane Thomas and Calvin Hill.

That's all background for what happened at Tulane Stadium on January 16, 1972.

Dallas was leading, 3-0, with halftime closing in when Staubach hit Alworth for a 21-yard gain. Hill ran for 25 yards over the next three snaps, setting up first-and-goal from the 7. Alworth's route took him a few steps into the end zone, all the way near the left sideline, and Staubach fired a dart. Alworth plucked it out of the air just before cornerback Curtis Johnson could get to it. The touchdown stretched the lead to 10-0.

Early in the fourth quarter, Dallas led, 17-3. The way Bob Lilly and the defense was having its way with Bob Griese and the Miami offense, this game was pretty much over—especially when Chuck Howley intercepted a pass and returned it 41 yards to the Miami 9-yard line.

On third-and-goal from the 7, Staubach lofted a pass toward the back right side of the end zone. Ditka was several steps ahead of his nearest pursuer and hopped to make the grab.

For Alworth, the catch that set up his touchdown and the touchdown itself were the only catches he ever made in the Super Bowl. Ditto for Ditka and his lone grab.

Staubach would go on to throw six more touchdowns in the Super Bowl, but never another to a future Hall of Famer.

10 Back in the rookie section, when writing about Dan Bailey, we described how much better kickers are today than in earlier years in the NFL. This entry shows just how badly the Cowboys struggled to find a reliable kicker.

They actually had a Pro Bowler in 1961. Only, he was honored for his play at tight end. Dick Bielski made 6-of-9 attempts after taking over for Allen Green, the rookie who won the first game in franchise history but who lost his job after making only 5-of-15 attempts.

The Cowboys had a carousel of kickers the next few years: Sam Baker, Dick Van Raaphorst, and Danny Villanueva. Eventually, the Cowboys set out to find someone more reliable.

Before the '67 season, personnel director Gil Brandt, kicking coach Ben Agajanian, and assistant coach Ermal Allen toured 28 cities in what was dubbed their "Kicking Karavan."

The 10,000-mile odyssey produced more laughs than anything else. Among them: the 60-year-old who made 15 straight 20-yarders; the bus driver who stopped his route, tried one kick, missed it, then got back behind the wheel and zoomed away; and the barefoot kicker whose toenails cut up the hands of a Cowboys staffer.

About 1,300 players tried out. They brought in 27 for a closer look. After all that, they stuck with Villanueva. (Note: Villanueva was pretty good in '65, a little less so in '66, and then quite unreliable in '67. He never played in the NFL again; instead, he went into television and did pretty well for himself: he co-founded the Univision network, selling it for $260 million in 1987. He died in 2015. He was seventy-seven.)

A few years later, the Cowboys decided to try again. By now, soccer-style kickers were becoming all the rage, so this time Brandt's expedition turned into a European vacation.

It started in Vienna. The very first candidate was Toni Fritsch, who was beloved in his native Austria as "Wembley Toni," because in 1966 he scored two goals in the national team's victory over England at Wembley Stadium, a feat made more significant by the fact that England won the World Cup that year.

The Cowboys had found their man.

In his first NFL game, Fritsch kicked a 26-yard field goal with 1:53 left to give Dallas a 16-13 victory over the St. Louis Cardinals. Cardinals linebacker Larry Stallings tried to rattle the rookie by screaming that he was going to choke. Dallas's Dave Edwards told Stallings to save his breath; Fritsch didn't understand much English.

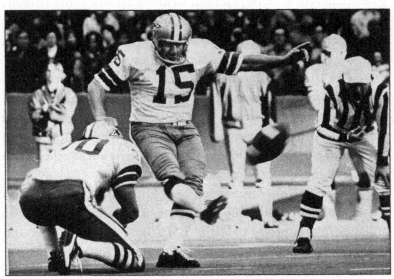

Austrian soccer great Toni Fritsch was the key find on the Cowboys' overseas "Kicking Karavan." He spent four seasons with the club. (AP Photo)

Fritsch split time with Mike Clark in '71, then was the primary kicker in 1972, '73, and '75. He led the NFC in field goals with 22 in 1975.

He later played for San Diego, Houston, and New Orleans. He was the league's most accurate kicker in 1977, '79, and '80 and made All-Pro in '79 with the "Luv Ya Blue" Oilers.

He was at his best in the postseason, making at least one field goal in 13 straight playoff games, a record that still stands.

Fritsch died in 2005. He was sixty.

11 Jimmy Johnson wanted to send a message.

The Cowboys roared into the 1992 season finale on a 9-2 roll, with the losses by a combined seven points. Things were clicking in every way. It was almost too good, at least from Johnson's perspective. He needed to keep everyone on their toes—to give them something to talk about and think about, beyond what size Super Bowl ring they'd need.

But, how? It was going to be tough, especially when the Cowboys were leading the Bears, 27-0, in the fourth quarter.

Emmitt Smith went out for good at that point, having already wrapped up his second straight rushing title with a club-record 1,713 yards. In went his backup, "Swervin'" Curvin Richards.

Richards fumbled, and the Bears cashed it in for a touchdown. Then he fumbled again, and Chicago returned it for another touchdown. The Cowboys still won easily, but now Johnson had his perfect sacrificial lamb.

Johnson cut Richards the next day.

Sloppy teams don't win championships. You've got to protect the ball. You can't give away points. Etc., etc. Those were the types of themes Johnson wanted to get across. It was reminiscent of Johnson's first training camp, when he relegated an injured player to the "asthma field" to send a message about his intolerance for guys who aren't tough enough.

"I want to go into the playoffs with people I can count on," Johnson said.

Some players saw through the charade. After all, Richards was about the least important player on the roster—the backup to a workhorse who wasn't likely to miss many snaps in the postseason. And he always was a lackadaisical character, the kind who was tough to count on.

There's no way of knowing whether this ploy kept guys focused. But you can't argue with the results: Dallas won it all that season and the next.

As for Richards, he made the Lions the next year—going from backing up Smith to backing up Barry Sanders. He carried the ball four times in the opener and gained just one yard. And that was it. His NFL career was done.

12 It was a running play called "Load Left", and when the Cowboys were clicking, it could've been announced over the stadium's public-address system and still worked. That's how good Emmitt Smith and his blockers were.

So coach Barry Switzer knew what he was doing by calling for *that* play.

The mind-boggling thing is the fact that he did it in *that* situation.

Even if the Cowboys had gotten the first down, they still would've been about 70 yards from the end zone. They needed about 35 yards just to get into the outer edge of field-goal territory. And if they failed to get the first down, Philadelphia would already be in field goal position.

With the game tied, punting was an overwhelmingly smart option. Give a defense featuring Charles Haley and Deion Sanders the chance to force overtime or maybe even get the ball back.

But Switzer had just seen the Eagles claw back from a 17-3 deficit. He also worried that stiff winds would keep a punt from traveling very far; punter John Jett already had shanked a 23-yarder in the quarter. (The temperature was 13 degrees at kickoff. At this point, with the wind chill, it felt like minus-7 degrees.)

All things considered, there's still no justifying the decision. Then again, Switzer's tenure as coach of the Cowboys would include several head-scratching decisions, like the time he packed a gun in his carry-on luggage and the time he ate three hot dogs during a game (OK, it was the Pro Bowl, but, still . . .).

Dallas ran the play, but it didn't work. It also didn't count.

Switzer was saved by the bell. The 2-minute warning went off, giving him a chance to come to his senses.

Nevertheless, he called the same play again. And it failed again. The Eagles kicked the game-winning field goal, and the anti-Switzer backlash was fierce as could be in a pre-Twitter world. There were lines like "Switzercide" and "Fourth-and-Dumb."

"The sequel to *Dumb and Dumber*," Mike Ditka said on television.

The *New York Post* called Switzer "Bozo the Coach." (Switzer liked that one so much he had it framed for his children.)

Here's the part of the story that often gets forgotten: the Cowboys never lost again that season.

Dallas won the final two games of the regular season, then rolled through the postseason to win a fifth Super Bowl. The playoff opener, by the way, was a 30-11 victory over the Eagles.

"We did it our way, bay-bee!" Switzer hollered as he held the Lombardi Trophy.

13 The list is more extensive than you might realize:

SITE	LOCATION	YEARS
Pacific University	Forest Grove, Oregon	1960
St. John's Military Academy	Delafield, Wisconsin	1960
St. Olaf College	Northfield, Minnesota	1961
Northern Michigan University	Marquette, Michigan	1962
California Lutheran College	Thousand Oaks, California	1963-89
St. Edward's University	Austin, Texas	1990-97
Midwestern State University	Wichita Falls, Texas	1998-2001
River Ridge Sports Complex	Oxnard, California	2001, 2004-06, 2008, 2010, 2012-15
Alamodome	San Antonio, Texas	2002-03, 2007, 2009-11

This traveling circus got started in Forest Grove, Oregon, because Tom Landry had trained at a university about 40 miles away while with his previous club, the New York Giants. He liked the Pacific Northwest climate and figured he would stick with what worked. It also made sense because Dallas's first-ever preseason game was in nearby Seattle.

Landry also liked the seclusion. He wanted players to focus on nothing but football, which was easier to do in a town with just one movie theater and one bar.

Landry ran a boot-camp-like environment, capped by what became known as the "Landry Mile." Skill players had to run a 6-minute mile; linemen got an extra 30 seconds. It proved to be a disaster—though not as bad as what happened when they moved east to Delafield, Wisconsin, for the last two weeks of camp.

In 1922, a team known as the Milwaukee Badgers prepared for their season at St. John's Military Academy in what's possibly the first instance of a pro football team holding an out-of-town training camp. The problem for the 1960 Cowboys was that the school's facilities were still pretty much as they'd been in the 1920s.

Personnel director Gil Brandt—who insisted that St. John's officials promised him that the place had recently been renovated—was hung in effigy.

The next year, the Cowboys headed to Northfield, Minnesota, a town best known as the site of a failed bank robbery by legendary outlaw Jesse James and his gang. Landry liked it there enough to try returning in '62, but the school's conference enacted a rule against pro teams on campus, so the Cowboys were left scrambling. They found Northern Michigan University—specifically, the unoccupied girls' dormitory. Let's just say the living conditions weren't ideal for burly football players. Plus, it came close to freezing at night.

In 1963, former Army star Glenn Davis was working for the *Los Angeles Times* as a director of special events. He was planning the city's annual charity football game and wanted the Cowboys in it. Tex Schramm agreed on the condition that Davis find him a place nearby to the train. He sent the team to California Lutheran University in Thousand Oaks, and the Cowboys were treated like kings compared to their recent experiences.

The Cowboys loved the weather and the folks on campus, and the community loved the Cowboys. The bond was so tight that in 1980, the school created The Landry Medal, an honor for those who inspire youngsters. Recipients included Roger Staubach, John Wooden, and Bob Hope. (The first recipient was *Peanuts* creator Charles M. Schulz; coincidentally, he and Landry died on the same day: February 12, 2000.)

Jerry Jones kept the Cowboys at Cal Lutheran his first season, then decided to set up shop closer to home. They spent eight years in Austin before heading east to Wichita Falls, where 100- degree practices were the norm. That got real old, real fast, prompting a return to Oxnard, although at a completely different facility (a series of fields connected to a Residence Inn previously used by the Raiders when they called Los Angeles home). A year later, the Cowboys came back to Texas but avoided the heat by going indoors at the Alamodome. Bill Parcells didn't like practicing on turf, so it was back to the hotel in Oxnard; it's pretty much been back-and-forth ever since. (There was one time when Jerry Jones tried growing grass on the concrete of the Alamodome parking lot. If it sounds like a terrible idea, the reality was even worse. Emmitt Smith took a few steps and refused to go any farther.)

The merry-go-round is likely to end soon with the Cowboys moving into a sprawling new team headquarters in the Dallas suburb of Frisco. (The city north of Dallas already is home to headquarters of the NHL's Dallas Stars, the Texas Rangers' Class AA affiliate, the Dallas Mavericks' NBA Development League team, and FC Dallas of the MLS. Yet the Cowboys will instantly be the kings of the area both because they're the Cowboys and because of the caliber of the facility they are building. Between the facility itself and the planned development around it—including a hotel—it would make sense for them to stick around there for training camp.)

14 Ralph Neely was a two-time All-America selection at Oklahoma, so teams from the NFL and AFL were eager to have him. The Baltimore Colts and Houston Oilers each drafted him.

Back then, each league held its 1965 draft in November 1964. And because they were fighting to sign the same players, secret deals (undated contracts) were routinely signed before players finished their college eligibility. Neely got one of those with the AFL's Oilers, collecting a signing bonus of $25,000. Then two things happened: the Cowboys traded for his NFL rights, and the Sooners found out about Neely's contract, declaring him ineligible for the Gator Bowl. Angry about the leak, Neely got revenge by returning the bonus and signing instead with the Cowboys. He figured that between the refunded money and the undated contract, he was in the clear.

A deal's a deal, though, and the Oilers still wanted Neely. So they asked the courts to enforce their contract—and to void his deal with Dallas. By the time it was resolved, Neely was already entrenched on the Cowboys.

Dallas actually won the first round of the legal battle, but Houston won an appeal. The Cowboys sought relief from the U.S. Supreme Court, but the highest court in the land apparently had more important things to do and didn't hear the case.

As all this played out, the NFL and AFL were trying to merge. The Neely case was among the holdups. The Cowboys and Oilers ended up settling their case. Neely stayed in Dallas, and the lawsuit was resolved with the following terms:

- In the 1967 draft—the first draft featuring the two leagues together—Houston got Dallas's first- and second-round picks, plus a pair of fifth-rounders.
- The Cowboys had to cover the Oilers' court costs.

- Dallas had to play an annual exhibition game against Houston, a meeting that would long be referred to as "The Ralph Neely Bowl."

The price was worth it to the Cowboys considering what a devastating force Neely was at right tackle back when that was the premiere position on the offensive line. Put it this way: he arrived in the NFL in 1965 and still made the All-Decade Team for the 1960s.

Neely moved to left tackle when Rayfield Wright emerged, giving Dallas an enviable set of bookends on its offensive line. The combination helped the Cowboys reach the Super Bowl following the 1970 season.

In 1971, Dallas was 4-3 at midseason. During the next off day, Neely joined a group of players to go riding and jumping motorcycles near Lake Grapevine, northwest of Dallas.

Bob Lilly, Cliff Harris, Charlie Waters, Mike Ditka, Dan Reeves, and Mike Edwards knew what they were doing. Neely didn't. To try keeping up, he bought a big, powerful bike, but that actually only made it tougher to control. (Teammates called Neely "Rotten" because nothing ever seemed good enough to him. For instance, his expensive bike was rotten because it kept toppling.)

The regulars were worn out from riding and ready to call it a day, but Neely—who was just starting to get the hang of it—asked to keep going. Harris offered to show Neely the way up a hill for a nice view of the lake.

Harris made it, then waited for Neely to follow.

After his first try up the incline failed, Neely generated more momentum the next time and made it easily. But when he arrived, he was going too fast to stop. The slope essentially turned into a ramp, launching him about 20 feet into the air.

As a novice, he didn't know how to handle the landing and broke his right leg in three places, ending his season.

As Neely recovered, so did the Cowboys from their slow start. Dallas won the rest of its games that season, including its first Super Bowl title. Neely got a ring but not the satisfaction of earning it. At a 40th anniversary celebration of that victory, he tearfully called it the biggest regret of his career. (The flip side to Neely's absence is that it turned Tony Liscio into a Super Bowl champion. Liscio had been the Cowboys' primary starting left tackle from 1963 to 1970, then was traded and ended up retiring. He'd been selling real estate in Dallas when Tom Landry lured him back.)

Neely returned in 1972 and remained a durable, quality starter at left tackle through the 1977 season. His final game? The Super Bowl victory over Denver.

15 Steve Beuerlein, the "bus driver" backup to Troy Aikman from the 1991 season, served that role again in 1992. After collecting a Super Bowl ring, he went to the Cardinals.

Jason Garrett began the 1993 season as Aikman's backup and even got to see some mop-up duty. Midway through the season, the Cleveland Browns surprisingly cut Bernie Kosar, and the Cowboys eagerly signed him. Aikman happened to have a hamstring injury at the time, so a more reliable backup just made sense.

Kosar could've signed anywhere but picked Dallas for the chance to win a Super Bowl. It also meant a reunion with Jimmy Johnson, for better or for worse.

Kosar led Miami to a national championship in 1983, the year before Johnson arrived as head coach. They were together for one season, before Kosar turned pro with two years of eligibility remaining. (He'd actually graduated.) Johnson and the

Hurricanes recovered from his departure, but Johnson and UM officials later showed how much it stung. In 1986, Johnson announced that the school was retiring the jersey of Kosar's successor, Vinny Testaverde—who won a Heisman Trophy, but not a national championship—yet refused to do the same for Kosar. A controversy ensued, with Kosar saying he cared less about the honor and more about Johnson's insinuation that he hurt the school by leaving early. Johnson then said Kosar's premature departure kept him from earning more accolades that would've warranted a retired jersey.

Ready for the twist? When Cleveland cut Kosar, Testaverde took his place. (The coach who did this and who later admitted he bungled it: Bill Belichick. Also, one more link in this chain of events—albeit minor and unrelated, but still interesting—is that Testaverde played for the Cowboys in 2004. More on that later in the book.)

Anyway, back to Kosar and the 1993 Cowboys.

Aikman's hamstring injury indeed kept him out the week that Kosar arrived. Garrett made his first career start but lasted only a few series. Johnson turned to Kosar, and he led Dallas to a 20-15 victory over the Cardinals. (Beuerlein, by the way, watched from the other sideline, as he'd already lost his starting job to Chris Chandler.)

Kosar started the next week, and the Cowboys lost to Atlanta. Then Aikman returned, and Kosar settled into the No. 2 job, until the third quarter of the NFC Championship game.

This was the game best remembered for Johnson's "put it in three-inch headlines" guarantee. Aikman led the Cowboys to a 21-point halftime lead, then took an accidental knee to the head. His brain was so foggy that he thought the next week's Super Bowl was going to be played in Henryetta, Oklahoma (his hometown). He also couldn't name the MVP of the previous Super Bowl (it was him). So, in went Kosar.

The 49ers came after him hard, and he responded just like the Cowboys hoped a veteran would. His big test came on a third-and-9 with Dallas leading, 28-14; he hit Michael Irvin for a 12-yard gain. Kosar went on to throw a touchdown pass while sending the Cowboys to a 38-21 victory and a trip to the Super Bowl. Johnson showed his appreciation to Kosar by letting him onto the field for the final snap, a kneel-down that sealed the 30-13 victory and the first and only Super Bowl ring of Kosar's career.

Nice ending, right? Well, the story continues.

Kosar went to the Dolphins the next year and remained there as Dan Marino's backup through the 1996 season. In case you haven't already guessed, his coach that season was Johnson. The Hurricanes, by the way, never did retire Kosar's jersey.

16 Here's how mesmerizing of a talent Duane Thomas was: The Cowboys took Calvin Hill in the first round of the 1969 draft, and he lived up to expectations by rushing for 942 yards, second-best in team history. Yet Dallas still spent its first-round pick in 1970 on Thomas, convinced he was even better. And he was, leading the team in rushing as a rookie with a rare blend of size and speed.

Thomas also had a mesmerizing personality. You may recall his famous line about the Super Bowl, uttered prior to the championship game following his rookie year: "How can it be the ultimate game if they play it next year, too?"

But Thomas's quirky character wasn't always an asset.

He wanted a raise after his rookie season but had practically no leverage. Tex Schramm also was fiercely cheap when it came to contracts and wasn't about to reward anyone for outplaying a contract if he didn't have to. So Thomas tried playing the only card he could. He retired.

The Cowboys just laughed. What else would Thomas do that would pay him nearly as much as playing football? Besides, even if he tried a lengthy holdout, they still had Hill.

A bizarre series of events followed, but nothing compared to what happened one July afternoon at the Dallas Press Club. (This was even more unusual because the team—and the main reporters who covered the team—were all at the Cowboys training camp in California.)

Wearing an African shirt called a dashiki, bell-bottom jeans, and sandals, Thomas outlined his contract demands, then threw out his famous screed: "Tex Schramm is sick, demented, and completely dishonest. Tom Landry is a plastic man, actually no man at all. Gil Brandt is a liar."

Thomas rambled for about 45 minutes. Soon after, a tape of the entire thing was played over the telephone to Schramm, Brandt, and Landry.

What did Schramm think of the personal attacks?

"Well," he said, "he got two out of three."

Thomas eventually returned and again led the team in rushing. But he hardly spoke to anyone—definitely not coaches and rarely even his teammates, thus drawing the nickname, "The Sphinx." Long before Marshawn Lynch harrumphed his way through a Super Bowl Media Day, Thomas went through his Super Bowl Media Day session saying only, "Leave me alone. I don't want to talk to anybody." When it was almost done, he uttered, "What time is it?"

Thomas ran 19 times for 95 yards and a touchdown in Dallas's victory over Miami in that Super Bowl. He could've been the MVP, but, as the story goes, the brass was concerned with how he'd handle the ceremony. (Would he show up? Would he speak? If so, what might he say?) So the honor instead went to Roger Staubach. (Here's how anti-establishment Staubach was: he was supposed to get a sports car as his prize but asked for—and received—a station wagon instead.)

That proved to be Thomas's final game for the Cowboys. He was traded to San Diego but never played for them. He played some for Washington in 1974 and '75, and played briefly in the World Football League.

17 Cornell Green was such a great basketball player at Utah State University that the school retired his jersey.

He was such a football novice that he didn't even know how to put on his uniform properly.

This was discovered when he complained of a hip problem. The root cause: he was wearing his hip pads upside down.

In one of his first preseason games, the raw rookie went up against the reigning Super Bowl champion Green Bay Packers. He forced a fumble and recovered it, proving to himself and others that he could make it in this sport.

Green arrived in 1962 and started at cornerback until 1970, when Dallas acquired future Hall of Famer Herb Adderley. Adderley took over at cornerback, and Green moved to strong safety. He retired after the 1974 season, having never missed a game in 13 seasons. His 34 career interceptions remain tied for fifth-most in team history. His four defensive touchdowns (two each on fumble and interception returns) were tops when he retired and are now tied for third-best.

Green became such a student of football that he went into scouting. In fact, he began doing that for the Cowboys during his playing days and continued in that role through 1979. He got back into scouting with the Broncos in 1987 and kept that job through May 2015. In 2010, he was named the AFC Scout of the Year. (One more tidbit: His older brother is Pumpsie Green, the first African-American to play for the Boston Red Sox. Pumpsie spent four seasons with the Red Sox and one with the Mets.)

18 The NFL draft is such a crapshoot that sometimes it's worth throwing things against the wall to see if they'll stick.

No, Riley didn't work out. But that late-round pick of Roger Staubach sure did. As did Tex Schramm's mid-round investment into Herschel Walker. And years after Schramm left the organization, the Cowboys cashed in on his late-round gamble on Chad Hennings.

Yet perhaps his most interesting roll of the draft dice came with the 334th pick (out of 336) in the 1984 draft.

From the University of Houston, the Cowboys selected wide receiver . . . Carl Lewis.

"We drafted the best athlete available in the 12th round and you can't do much better than that," said Greg Aiello, the team spokesman at the time, now the NFL's vice president of communications.

The draft was held prior to the 1984 Summer Olympics in Los Angeles, when Lewis won three gold medals as a sprinter and another as a long jumper. Instead of following the sprinter-to-Cowboys-starter trail blazed by "Bullet" Bob Hayes, who became the "world's fastest human" at the 1964 Olympics, Lewis stuck with track and field. He went on to win 10 Olympic medals and accolades as the greatest Olympian of the 20th century.

A few months after the Cowboys drafted Lewis, so did the Chicago Bulls. He was their 10th-round pick in the same draft during which they selected Michael Jordan in the first round.

19 The Belles & Beaux were troupes of local teenagers—high school kids—who did the old-fashioned, rah-rah type of cheers through megaphones. They prowled the sidelines at the Cotton Bowl throughout the 1960s and even into the 1971 season, when the Cowboys moved into Texas Stadium and won their first championship.

Then Tex Schramm came up with another idea, one that involved older and, uh, more physically mature ladies.

The concept began with female ushers known as "Texettes." They wore a cowboy hat, skirt, and cowboy-themed attire. On the original newspaper ads, applicants were recommended to "please wear shorts or minis. Bring heels."

Their popularity helped spawn the cheerleaders the next year, 1972.

20 Jesse Holley was a backup point guard on the North Carolina team that won the NCAA championship in 2005. A few months later, he gave up basketball to focus on football.

Holley played football for all four years with the Tar Heels, leading the team in catches and yards as a junior. He was so serious about making it in football that he got a tattoo with the words "Heavenly Received" around a pair of steepled hands wearing football receiver gloves.

In 2007, Holley spent about a month on the Cincinnati Bengals practice squad before they cut him. He latched on with the B.C. Lions of the Canadian Football League the next year but was released after a single preseason game.

In 2009, Holley's godfather told him he couldn't hang onto his dream much longer. Holley—who was working as a security guard and selling cell phones—decided to give football one final shot. Around that time, Spike TV announced plans for *4th and Long*, its reality show pitting NFL wannabes, with the winner guaranteed the 80th and final spot on the Cowboys' training camp roster.

Holley made the pool of 12 contestants: six receivers and six defensive backs. They all lived in the Cotton Bowl. Former Cowboys assistant coach Joe Avezzano guided the receivers, and former Cowboys defensive back Bill Bates guided the defensive backs. When it came time for the final choice, Irvin took the tall receiver with the bright smile.

The TV show only earned Holley a chance. The rest was up to him, and he made the most of it.

After spending 2009 on the practice squad, he made the roster in 2010. He played in 12 games, all on special teams.

Holley made the club again in 2011. And in the second game, against San Francisco, Holley trotted out with the offense for what turned out to be the final drive of the fourth quarter.

Trailing, 24-21, with 4:03 left, Tony Romo opened the drive with consecutive passes to Holley—an 11-yarder, then an 8-yarder. They were the first two receptions of his career. The drive ended with a field goal as time expired, forcing overtime.

The 49ers got the ball first and punted it to Dallas. On the first play, Romo faked a handoff and looked to pass. The safety who was responsible for Holley had gone for the fake, and Romo saw it. He threw deep to Holley for a 77-yard gain, one yard shy of the game-ending touchdown. The Cowboys immediately kicked a field goal for the victory.

Holley caught only four more passes that season, finishing with seven catches for 169 yards. Still, it's pretty good for a guy discovered on a reality TV show.

RING OF HONOR LEVEL

This is it, the pinnacle of achievement for a Dallas Cowboys player.* Your name is emblazoned inside the stadium, forever facing the field—in full view of every player, coach, and fan who walks into the building. This distinction goes to the upper 1 percent of the upper 1 percent, much like these questions, which are designed for the most devoted, knowledgeable fans.

1 Thanks to Roger Staubach and Troy Aikman, the job of quarterback of the Dallas Cowboys is arguably the most high-profile in all of sports. Yet in the span between Aikman's last start and Tony Romo's first, the shine faded. The job instead became a revolving door of guys supposedly on their way up and others who supposedly had something left on their way down. *Answer on page 171.*

   • How many were there? How many can you name?
   • Can you put them in order of appearance based on their first start?
   • Who won the most games?

---

* Yes, a bust in the Pro Football Hall of Fame is the ultimate recognition of greatness. But that requires a trip to Canton, Ohio, to see it. The Ring of Honor is essentially the team's Hall of Fame, on permanent display on the team's home turf.

2 Because of the status that comes with being the starting quarterback for the Dallas Cowboys, even doing it once has to be quite a thrill. *Answer on page 175.*

- How many quarterbacks started exactly one game for the Cowboys? How many can you name?
- Which went 1-0?
- Which went 0-1?

3 Emmitt Smith and Tony Dorsett lead the list of Cowboys who ran for 1,000 yards in a season, but they're far from the only players who've done it. *Answer on page 178.*

- How many have done it? How many can you name?
- Which did so multiple times?
- Bonus: name the player who got to 975 yards during a season in which he didn't start a single game.

4 Knowing details of the careers of Emmitt Smith and Tony Dorsett is one thing. Appreciating the exploits of Calvin Hill and Duane Thomas shows another level of knowledge. But only Ring of Honor-caliber fans can remember the following ball carriers who had only brief moments in the spotlight. *Answer on page 180.*

- He's the first player to lead the team in rushing for a full season.
- His shining moment came during a memorable Thanksgiving game. Alas, it was the Thanksgiving game best remembered for Leon Lett's flub that turned a sure win into a loss.
- After three seasons as a backup, he became the starter by default after Smith's departure. He led the team in rushing, then joined Smith in Arizona.

5 Tom Landry had an eye for talent on the sideline as well as the field. Of his many assistant coaches, how many went on to become head coaches in the NFL? *Answer on page 183.*
- How many can you name?
- Who won the most games?
- Who won the most Super Bowls?

6 The Cowboys have resided in the NFC East ever since the division was created in 1970, following the merger of the NFL and AFL and the formation of conferences. That leaves 10 seasons played in divisions of a different name. *Answer on page 185.*
- What were those other names?
- Which years did they play in each of those divisions?
- The inaugural season was the only one in which the Redskins and Eagles were not division foes. How many of the rivals in that division can you name?

7 Who am I? *Answer on page 186.*
- As a rookie with the Detroit Lions in 1951, I started at defensive end. Two years later, while still starting at defensive end, I'd also become an accomplished offensive end—that era's term for what we now call a receiver. In fact, I caught a 33-yard touchdown pass from Bobby Layne to give the Lions a 17-16 victory in the 1953 NFL Championship game. I was Detroit's leading receiver in 1957, when the Lions won it all again.
- After the 1959 season, the Lions left me available to be taken in the expansion draft. The Cowboys snagged me, although not until their 12th pick.

- I proved to be quite a find. Not only did I score the first touchdown in team history, but I also became the first Pro Bowl selection in team history.

8 Jersey No. 88 is synonymous with great Cowboys receivers. Drew Pearson started the tradition, Michael Irvin emblazoned it, and Dez Bryant brought it into a new era. Yet they aren't the only guys to wear it. *Answer on page 188.*
  - Not counting that trio, how many other players have worn No. 88?
  - How many can you name? (Hint: it's an eclectic mix that includes a pair of tight ends, a punter, and even a linebacker.)

9 The Heisman Trophy is the most prestigious individual award in college football. How many Heisman winners have played for the Cowboys? *Answer on page 191.*
  - How many can you name?
  - Can you name their schools?
  - Do you know what years they won the Heisman?

10 The club record for Super Bowl appearances by a player is five, done by several guys. *Answer on page 192.*
  - How many Cowboys have done it?
  - How many can you name?
  - Bonus: Several other players in NFL history have five Super Bowl appearances, including two guys who each appeared in three Super Bowls with the Cowboys. Can you name them?

RING OF HONOR
LEVEL – ANSWERS

1 Midway through the first quarter of a home game against the Redskins on December 10, 2000, the Cowboys faced third-and-goal from the Washington 1-yard line.

Troy Aikman rolled right and threw the ball toward James McKnight in the end zone. As Aikman threw the pass—which would fall incomplete—Redskins linebacker LaVar Arrington knocked the quarterback to the turf . . . so hard that it would be the final play of his career.

For the first time in his tenure as owner of the Dallas Cowboys, Jerry Jones had to find a new starting quarterback.

Six years and eight failed experiments later, Jones finally found his guy in Tony Romo.

The frustration of those in-between years was best summed up by Bill Parcells during training camp in 2004.

"You know what I like about the media? They think you can just dial 1-800 and get a quarterback," Parcells said. "There are teams that have been trying to dial that for 10 years. . . . You think we don't look around? You act like someone is not trying."

Trying? Yes.

Succeeding? No.

Dallas won just 38 of the 88 games between the eras. The whole thing could best be summed up by the fact that Quincy Carter had the most starts and won the most games.

Here are the gory details:

NAME	FIRST START	RECORD
Anthony Wright	Dec. 17, 2000	1-4
Quincy Carter	Sept. 9, 2001	16-15
Clint Stoerner	Oct. 28, 2001	1-1
Ryan Leaf	Nov. 11, 2001	0-3
Chad Hutchinson	Oct. 27, 2002	2-7
Vinny Testaverde	Sept. 12, 2004	5-10
Drew Henson	Nov. 25, 2004	1-0
Drew Bledsoe	Sept. 11, 2005	12-10

Here are thumbnail sketches of each "era":

- When Aikman went down, Wright was already the backup. He took over against the Redskins and started the last two games of the 2000 season. He lost both. In the finale, a 31-0 loss to Tennessee, he had a quarterback rating of 0.0. He earned it by completing 5-of-20 passes for 35 yards with two interceptions. He still managed to get three more starts the next year, logging a rating of 21.8 in one of them.
- Jones was smitten by Carter—or, rather, the idea of him. Having seen the success of late-round pick Tom Brady and other quarterbacks not taken near the top of the draft, Jones dreamed that the former baseball player coming off a dismal junior year at the University of Georgia would be his long-term solution. He was so sure of it that he traded up to grab Carter in the second round, even though all projections had him going in the third round or later. About the nicest thing to say about him is that he wasn't terrible. But he didn't have any great skills, either—not throwing, not running, and certainly not decision-making. Carter also

wasn't much of a leader and had a strange tendency of comparing his early career struggles with the fact that Aikman started 0-11. Carter went 3-5 as a rookie in 2001 and 3-4 the next year. Parcells coaxed a 10-6 campaign from him in 2003 but dumped Carter afterward. Imagine what the market would be today for a twenty-six-year-old coming off a playoff season. The best Carter could do was land on the New York Jets as a backup. He started three more games, then was out of the NFL. He bounced all over the fringes of pro football, even indoor football's minor league.

- Stoerner set a bunch of passing records at Jones's alma mater, the University of Arkansas and beat the Longhorns in the Cotton Bowl. So once he went undrafted, Jones signed him. Perhaps the most memorable aspect of his career is the fact that he lost his roster spot in 2003 to another undrafted quarterback—Romo. But, wait—Stoerner actually won a game, beating the Arizona Cardinals in his first career start. How? Credit a Dallas defense that gave up only a field goal while providing a touchdown on an interception return.

- Leaf had been the No. 2 pick of the 1998 draft; there actually had been a debate over whether he or Peyton Manning should go No. 1. But his fall to major-bust status was already underway when Jones gave him a chance. In three starts, Leaf threw more touchdowns for the opponents (two) than he did for the Cowboys (one). He never played in the NFL again.

- Hutchinson made it to the major leagues as a pitcher, getting in three games for the St. Louis Cardinals in 2001. His ERA was 24.75, bad enough to prompt him to give football a try. Once again, Jones tried to find a bargain.

Once again, it backfired. His first start came in the game when Emmitt Smith became the all-time rushing king. Thanks in part to Hutchinson, Dallas lost that game. He's perhaps best remembered for his training camp battle with Carter in 2003, when HBO's *Hard Knocks* cameras showed him asking Parcells to give him a clear definition of his role. The answer: deep reserve. The only time he played that season was mop-up duty of a single game, a blowout win, before getting released after the season.

- Testaverde was forty when he came to Dallas, forty-one by season's end. The Cowboys were so desperate that they let him start nearly every game that season. A year after making the playoffs, Dallas went 6-10. Yet of everybody on this list, Testaverde may have contributed the most: Romo was a third-stringer in his second season, and he studied everything Testaverde did, from the weight room and practice field to watching film and taking notes in meetings. Romo credits Testaverde with teaching him how to be a starting quarterback in the NFL.
- Henson was yet another former baseball player, a guy once predicted to be the next big star for the New York Yankees. Instead, he's best remembered as the guy who started ahead of Tom Brady at the University of Michigan. His lone Dallas start came on Thanksgiving against Chicago. The game was tied at 7 at halftime, with the Bears scoring on the return of an intercepted Henson pass. Parcells sent out Testaverde for the second half, and he pulled out a 21-7 victory.
- Bledsoe was essentially a younger version of Testaverde— a guy whose greatest attribute at this point in his career was the fact that he'd once been good for Parcells. His 2005 numbers (3,639 yards, 23 touchdowns) were the

best of any quarterback in this stretch. But in 2006, his ratio of eight interceptions to seven touchdowns underscored how much his skills were slipping. Parcells knew Bledsoe well enough to realize the end of his career was rapidly approaching . . . and Parcells knew Romo well enough to realize the start of something may be brewing, too.

2 The Dallas Cowboys went into the 2016 season having played 850 games.

Of those, 630 were started by just six guys: Troy Aikman, Roger Staubach, Danny White, Tony Romo, Don Meredith, and Craig Morton.

The other 220 games were spread among 33 quarterbacks. Eleven of them started only a single game. Some of the names may surprise you for having only one start. Others may leave you wondering, "Who's he?"

Let's start with the five guys who went won-and-done:

- Clint Longley, 1975
- Glenn Carano, 1981
- Rodney Peete, 1994
- Drew Henson, 2004
- Stephen McGee, 2010

And now the 0-1 club:

- Don Heinrich, 1960
- Reggie Collier, 1986
- Babe Laufenberg, 1990
- Bernie Kosar, 1993
- Wade Wilson, 1996
- Kyle Orton, 2013

(Since we're on the subject of quarterbacks with perfect records one way or another, here are a few more. The only other quarterback never to lose a start for Dallas was Steve Beuerlein during his 4-0 run in 1991. Several guys failed to win despite multiple starts: Kellen Moore, 0-2; Ryan Leaf, 0-3; John Roach and Brandon Weeden, 0-4.)

Let's look at the most notable one-start wonders, beginning with Heinrich's appearance during the inaugural season.

From 1954-59, Heinrich did a decent job as a sometimes starter for the New York Giants. His record was 20-10-2, but he completed only 41.5 percent of his passes and had more interceptions than touchdowns. Still, the defensive coach of that squad—Tom Landry—thought enough of Heinrich to bring him to Dallas in the expansion draft. Landry considered having him groom Don Meredith, at least until he talked Eddie LeBaron into doing so. Yet on November 13, 1960, Landry had Heinrich start against Green Bay. The powerful Packers—whose coach, Vince Lombardi, had been Heinrich's offensive coach on the Giants—rolled past Dallas, 41-7. Heinrich was 5-of-13 for 55 yards and an interception. He left the Cowboys after that season, resurfacing again for one start with the Raiders in 1962; he lost.

Longley's one start is not the game he's best known for; in that one—on Thanksgiving 1974 against the Redskins—he came off the bench after Roger Staubach was injured. The one time he got the nod was the final game of the following season, when Dallas had its playoff spot secured and Staubach was better off resting. Longley led Dallas to a 31-21 victory over the New York Jets, keeping alive momentum that would carry the Cowboys all the way to the Super

Bowl, where they lost to the Pittsburgh Steelers. Against the Jets, Longley went 6-of-15 for 94 yards with a touchdown and an interception.

Carano's lone start was so unique that it became the subject of *My One and Only*, a half-hour episode of NFL Films Presents that aired in 2014. What made the game so compelling was that it was the one and only NFL start by both Carano and the opposing quarterback, David Humm of the Baltimore Colts. Wilder still, both were from Nevada, knew each other while in high school, and remained friends two decades later. (Adding to the drama, Humm was battling multiple sclerosis.) As for the game, Dallas won, 37-13, with Carano going 7-of-18 for 51 yards with a touchdown and an interception. He played two more seasons in Dallas, then left for the short-lived USFL. More recently, he's been known as the father of MMA fighter Gina Carano.

Collier is now thought of as someone ahead of his time, the first quarterback who could throw as well as he could run, and run as well as he could throw. But the league wasn't ready for someone like that. The Cowboys drafted him in the sixth round in 1983 (the draft famous for its standout quarterbacks) but wanted him to play receiver. He went to the USFL instead, then signed with Dallas after the rival league went out of business. In the 1986 season finale, he started against Chicago, going 4-of-9 for 44 yards and two interceptions, and running five times for 32 yards. The noteworthy part of his outing was that he became the first African-American starting quarterback in team history. He played two games for the Steelers as a replacement player during the 1987 strike and later had stints in the Arena Football League.

Laufenberg's big opportunity came in 1990, when the Cowboys were one year removed from bottoming out at 1-15 yet went into late December with a chance to make the playoffs. Then Aikman went down in the second-to-last game. Laufenberg took over and threw four interceptions. The Cowboys had little choice but to start him in the season finale. Laufenberg went 10-of-24 for 129 yards with a touchdown and two interceptions in a 26-7 loss to Atlanta, and Dallas had to wait another year to get into the playoffs. Things eventually worked out for Laufenberg, as he's become a beloved color man on the team's radio broadcasts.

Six years after Aikman and Peete battled as the starting quarterbacks for crosstown rivals UCLA and USC, they were starter and backup on the Cowboys in 1994. On November 20, Aikman got hurt against Washington, and Peete took over—until he sprained the thumb on his passing hand. That's what led to Jason Garrett's having his breakout game against the Packers on Thanksgiving 1994. By the time Dallas played again, Peete was healthy enough to return. He went 10-of-17 for 172 yards with one touchdown and an interception in a 31-19 victory over Philadelphia. Eager to be a starter again, he left the Cowboys and became the top quarterback in Philadelphia the next year. He played nine seasons in the NFL after leaving Dallas.

3 In 26 of their 56 seasons, the Cowboys have had a 1,000-yard rusher.

Emmitt Smith and Tony Dorsett combined for 19 of those.

That leaves only seven 1,000-yard seasons by anyone else. And two of those guys did it twice, so the real answer is that only five Dallas players—other than the two Hall of Famers—have cracked the milestone:

PLAYER	YEAR	RUSHING YARDS
DeMarco Murray	2014	1,845
Herschel Walker	1988	1,514
Calvin Hill	1973	1,142
DeMarco Murray	2013	1,121
Darren McFadden	2015	1,089
Julius Jones	2006	1,084
Calvin Hill	1972	1,036

Hill was the first in franchise history to crack 1,000 yards. So his 1972 tally was a franchise record, one he broke the next season.

Walker's big season is fifth-best in team history. It came during the three-season gap between the end of Dorsett's reign and the start of Smith's. (Walker also led the team in rushing in '87 with 891 yards. In 1989, it was Paul Palmer with a paltry 446, the least for a single-season leader since the inaugural season.)

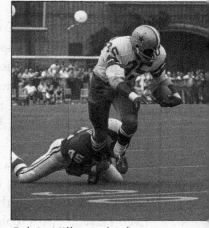

Calvin Hill was the first 1,000-yard rusher in team history. (AP Photo/ Bill Ingraham)

Murray's huge season is tops in team history, as detailed earlier in this book. Notice that he made the list the year before and that Darren McFadden made it the year after, once Murray left as a free agent. That's a good indication of the caliber of the offensive line they ran behind.

Jones's lone 1,000-yard season raises another interesting point: the lack of a running threat during the prime of Tony Romo's career. Jones's big season came the year that Romo replaced Drew Bledsoe. Romo wouldn't have a 1,000-yard runner behind him again until Murray in 2013.

The closest anyone came in that stretch was in 2007, when Marion "The Barbarian" Barber ran for 975 yards and 10 touchdowns. Barber didn't start a game that season but still made the Pro Bowl. (Jones, meanwhile, started and ran for 588 yards that season. Barber became the featured runner the next few seasons and wouldn't rush for as many yards again.)

4 From the start, the Cowboys were built to be a running team. This was evidenced by spending the very first pick in their expansion draft on running back L.G. "Long Gone" DuPre.

If only his performance had been as good as his nickname.

While DuPre led the club in rushing that season, he did so with a mere 362 yards. He gained 60 more the next season, before retiring.

DuPre had been a star at Baylor, then a third-round pick of the Baltimore Colts in 1955. He started in the 1958 NFL Championship game, the one known as "The Greatest Game Ever Played," with Baltimore beating the New York Giants in overtime. While DuPre ran for just 30 yards on 11 carries and caught two passes for seven yards, perhaps he made a good impression on the Giants' defensive coach: Tom Landry. Injuries limited DuPre the next season, keeping him out of the lineup when the Colts again beat Landry and the Giants in the championship game, and Baltimore made him available in the expansion draft.

DuPre started only five games for Dallas in 1960. Don McIlhenny was the first starter at running back and scored the first rushing touchdown in team history (a 5-yarder in the opener against the Steelers). McIlhenny's 321 yards rushing that season were second-best on the club; he was released early the next season.

DuPre's most important game came in the second-to-last game, when he ran for a touchdown and caught two touchdown passes to help the Cowboys tie the Giants, 31-31. His most productive rushing game was the finale, when he gained 83 yards.

DuPre died in 2001. He was sixty-eight.

(Note: Don Perkins was supposed to be the featured running back in 1960. The Cowboys were so eager to have him that—just like Don Meredith—Perkins received a "personal services" contract before the franchise officially came into existence. Perkins missed 1960 because of a foot injury suffered in the College All-Star Game. He led the team in rushing the next five years and seven of the eight that he played. He was among the NFL's top 10 in rushing each of those eight seasons and made the Pro Bowl six times. He and Meredith both retired after the 1968 season, and they went into the Ring of Honor together in 1976, the second and third selections.)

Lincoln Coleman is the running back whose big moment was eclipsed by Leon Lett's big flub.

Coleman grew up in Dallas and went on to play at Notre Dame. When coaches wanted to move him from running back, he transferred to Baylor. NFL teams barely gave him a look.

But Coleman wanted to keep playing football, so he played for a semipro team and then for the Dallas Texans of the Arena Football League. He paid his bills by working at The Home Depot.

Cowboys trainer Kevin O'Neill happened to catch a Texans game. He was impressed by Coleman and passed along the name to Cowboys running backs coach Joe Brodsky, who ended up inviting Coleman for a tryout. Talk about a pinch-me moment: signed on his birthday, Coleman then went on the practice field as part of the reigning Super Bowl champions and the team he grew up watching.

Coleman was inactive the first nine games of the 1993 season. The second game he suited up for was Thanksgiving against the Dolphins. Emmitt Smith had bruised a thigh the previous week and was iffy; the icy conditions made it risky to use him too much. So in the second quarter, Jimmy Johnson sent in Coleman for his NFL debut.

He ran six times for 41 yards on the drive, which ended with a touchdown pass. It was Dallas's only offensive touchdown of the game, and this out-of-nowhere rookie was largely responsible for it.

As far as highlights go, that was about it. Coleman played in only five more games that season and got carries in eight more the next year. His career totals: 98 carries, 312 yards, and three touchdowns.

The Cowboys cut him in 1995, and he latched on with the Falcons but never played for them. He went back to the Arena Football League, helping the Grand Rapids Rampage win the championship in 2001.

Troy Hambrick is another single-season sensation, although he wasn't very sensational.

Undrafted, the most interesting thing about his arrival on the Cowboys was that his older brother, Darren Hambrick, was a starting linebacker. Troy spent three seasons in Daryl

Johnston's old role of blocking back for Smith and occasional ball carrier. Then Smith was cut, and Hambrick was handed the starting job.

Playing behind Quincy Carter in the first season under Bill Parcells, Hambrick rumbled for 972 yards as the Cowboys went 10-6 and made the playoffs. His biggest highlight was a 189-yard performance against the Redskins; it was the third-best single game in team history. Yet Hambrick was basically a plodder, as evidenced by his average of 3.5 yards per carry that season.

Dallas drafted Julius Jones the following spring and got rid of Hambrick. He wound up in Arizona, again backing up Smith. A year later, Hambrick was out of the NFL.

5 Mike Ditka and Dan Reeves went from playing for Tom Landry to coaching under him to blossoming into the most successful branches of the "Tom Landry Head-Coaching Tree."

Ditka went 121-95 over 14 years with Chicago and New Orleans. His 1985 Bears team is considered among the greatest of all time—and their Super Bowl championship is the lone title won by a Landry-spawned coach.

Reeves spent 23 years guiding Denver, Atlanta, and the New York Giants. He went 190-165-2 and reached four Super Bowls. Going into the 2016 season, Reeves was No. 9 on the career wins list and tied for the fourth-most conference titles.

Other head coaches groomed by Landry:

- Dick Nolan (69-82-5 over 11 years with San Francisco and New Orleans)
- Raymond Berry (48-39 over six years with New England)

Of the many future head coaches spawned by Tom Landry, Mike Ditka (89) is the only one to win a Super Bowl, doing so with the 1985 Bears. (AP Photo)

- John Mackovic (30-34 over four years in Kansas City)
- Gene Stallings (23-34-1 over four years with St. Louis/Phoenix Cardinals)

In 1986, Ditka, Reeves, Berry, Mackovic, and Stallings were all head coaches—as, of course, was Landry. So six of a possible 28 coaches in the league that season were connected through "the man in the funny hat."

A few more details:

- Nolan's 49ers teams were a win away from reaching the Super Bowls after the 1970 and '71 seasons. Landry's Cowboys knocked them out both times.

184

- Berry was among the greatest receivers of his generation before retiring with plans to enter the business world. Then Landry called and talked Berry into becoming the Cowboys' passing game coordinator. Berry went on to guide the New England Patriots to their first Super Bowl, where they got steamrolled by Ditka's Bears. That's right—two members of the Landry coaching tree squared off in a Super Bowl.
- Two other guys could be declared as residing in the shade of the Landry tree. Ron Meyer was a Dallas scout years before becoming New England's head coach (Berry, by the way, replaced him), and Jim Shofner was a Landry assistant who became interim coach for Cleveland for seven games.

6 When the AFL and NFL merged in 1967, each kept their name. In 1970, they rebranded under a single flag—NFL—with the former leagues becoming known as conferences—AFC and NFC. And within those conferences came a new set of divisions. Dallas landed in the NFC East and has remained there.

When you look back at the annual standings from 1960-69, here is where you will find the Cowboys:

YEAR	NFL DIVISION	DIVISION RIVALS
1960	West	Bears, Colts, 49ers, Lions, Packers, Rams
1961-65	East	Browns, Cardinals, Eagles, Giants, Redskins, Steelers
1966	East	Browns, Cardinals, Eagles, Falcons, Giants, Redskins, Steelers
1967	Capital	Eagles, Redskins, Saints
1968	Capital	Eagles, Giants, Redskins
1969	Capital	Eagles, Redskins, Saints

Why the "Capital" division? The league was into seven-letter words that started with the letter *C*, as the other divisions were the Century, Coastal, and Central. While geographically they belonged in the Central, they were sticking in the same division as the Redskins, and obviously Washington, D.C., was the reason for the name Capital division.

When the NFC East was established, it grouped the Cowboys, Eagles, Giants, Redskins, and St. Louis Cardinals. The Cardinals remained a division foe through 2001, then shifted to the NFC West when the arrival of expansion teams prompted realignment to four-team divisions.

Interestingly, only four current NFC teams haven't been Dallas's divisional rivals over the years: the Vikings, Buccaneers, Seahawks, and Panthers.

Going into the 2016 season, the NFC East was the most successful division since the 1970 alignment. Its members combined for 20 Super Bowl trips and 12 titles.

7 Scoring the Cowboys' first touchdown and being the team's first Pro Bowler are pretty cool distinctions. Jim Doran had a lot of those in his career.

When he was growing up in tiny Beaver, Iowa, there were no football teams, so he played baseball and basketball. He took up football while attending Buena Vista College in 1947. Then he went to Iowa State University and quickly found the spotlight.

His eight catches for 203 yards against Oklahoma in a 1949 game set a national record. He finished that season with 34 catches for 689 yards, shattering the Big Seven Conference's record. He followed that with 42 catches for 652 yards and six touchdowns as a senior, which also earned him a nod as an All-American. He left Iowa State owning practically every receiving record for the school and conference.

The Lions liked him more as a defensive end, and he started there as a rookie in 1951. He dabbled at receiver, too, catching between 6 and 10 passes over each of his first three seasons.

A high point came in the 1953 NFL Championship game against the Cleveland Browns.

The Lions were trailing, 16-10, when they took over at their 20-yard-line with only a few minutes left. Doran told quarterback Bobby Layne that he could beat cornerback Warren Lahr on a deep ball, and Layne filed it away.

The drive opened with a 17-yard completion to Doran and was kept alive by an 18-yard connection to Doran on a third-and-10. Three plays later, the ball was on the Cleveland 33, and Layne asked Doran whether he still thought he could beat Lahr.

"Just throw it," Doran said. "I'll beat him."

Layne threw it, and Doran caught it about 10 yards past Lahr, scoring the touchdown that was capped by an extra point from Doak Walker, all of which gave Detroit the championship.

Doran caught 38 passes for 552 yards in 1955 and in '57 had 33 catches for 624 yards and five touchdowns. Those were pretty good numbers back then—enough to finish in the top 10 in the NFL for receptions. He was sixth in the league for receiving yards in '57.

His numbers plummeted in 1959, so the Lions made him available for the expansion draft. The Cowboys snatched him and turned him into a tight end.

Doran secured his spot in team lore with the 75-yard touchdown in the first quarter of the first game. He added a

54-yard touchdown in the fourth quarter of that game. (The Cowboys lost, 35-28, to Pittsburgh. The Steelers' quarterback that day? Bobby Layne.)

Doran caught only one more touchdown pass all season but still finished with team-best totals of 31 catches and 554 yards. The next year, he dipped to 13 catches for 153 yards, then was done as a player. He spent two years as an assistant coach in Detroit before leaving football for farming in Iowa.

Doran died in 1994. He was sixty-six.

8 The Cowboys don't retire jerseys. The closest they've come is refusing to issue No. 74 to anyone since Bob Lilly and No. 12 to anyone since Roger Staubach.

Instead, there's been some nice lineage—such as Bob Hayes and Emmitt Smith each forging Hall of Fame careers inside No. 22.

And, of course, there's No. 88, which Tex Schramm gave to Michael Irvin in hopes that he would pick up where Drew Pearson left off; then Jerry Jones did the same for Dez Bryant.

Plenty of others have worn 88, although you'd need an incredible memory to recall some of them:

NAME	POSITION	SEASONS
Sonny Davis	Linebacker	1961
Colin Ridgway	Punter	1965
Sonny Randle	Receiver	1968
Reggie Rucker	Receiver	1970-71
Ron Sellers	Receiver	1972
Jackie Harris	Tight end	2000-01
Antonio Bryant	Receiver	2002-04
Brett Pierce	Tight end	2005

Davis was a fourth-round pick out of Baylor University in 1961—and, thus, the fourth overall draft pick in team history. He played receiver in college, which might explain his choosing this jersey number despite being moved to linebacker. The experiment apparently failed, as his NFL career lasted just two games.

Ridgway is even more of an oddity: A high jumper for Australia in the 1956 Summer Olympics, he failed to make the team again in 1960 and came to the United States to attend the school now known as Lamar University. He became the first Australian to play in the NFL when he debuted in 1965, but his entire career lasted just three games, as his Australian Rules Football style proved to be a poor fit. He averaged 39.2 yards on 13 punts and remained in Dallas after his career. In 1993, he was murdered in his home. The case remains unsolved.

Randle is another guy who had a blink-and-you-missed-it tenure. While he played six games, he caught just one pass for 12 yards. But he was the first proven player to wear No. 88, as he'd been a four-time Pro Bowler for the Cardinals and once led the league in receiving touchdowns.

Rucker finished second in the NFL in catches one season and sixth another season. However, those came for the Patriots and Browns. For the Cowboys, he caught a mere 10 passes for 219 yards and two touchdowns over nine games. Yet his timing in Dallas was good: he started in the team's first Super Bowl. (One pass went his way, but it wasn't caught.)

Sellers had a great rookie season with the Patriots in 1969 and had a decent year for the Cowboys in '72, catching 31 passes for 653 yards and five touchdowns. His biggest contribution came in a first-round playoff game, when he caught a last-minute touchdown pass to beat the 49ers, 30-28, in one of Roger Staubach's greatest comeback wins. That play goes down as the first memorable connection between Staubach and No. 88, as Pearson slipped into that jersey the next year. (Sellers got traded to Miami the next season, playing in just three games as the Dolphins won their second straight Super Bowl.)

Nobody but Pearson and Irvin wore the number until Harris, a tight end who'd been a solid player for the Packers, Buccaneers, and Titans. He played for Tennessee in the Super Bowl following the 1999 season, then came to Dallas for Troy Aikman's final season. Harris caught two touchdowns from Aikman, adding to the legacy of the connection between Nos. 8 and 88. Over two years with the Cowboys, Harris caught 54 passes for 447 yards and seven touchdowns.

Antonio Bryant had the talent to continue the lineage years before Dez Bryant (no relation) arrived. A winner of college football's award for the top receiver as just a sophomore at the University of Pittsburgh, he turned pro after his junior year, and Dallas drafted him in the second round. He slid that far because of questions about his character. Work ethic and attitude proved to be his undoing; angrily throwing his No. 88 jersey in the face of coach Bill Parcells during a practice didn't help. Over 37 games with Dallas, he caught 99 passes for 1,549 yards and eight touchdowns.

Pierce, a tight end, wore No. 49 while Bryant had 88, then upgraded to this vaunted number for one season. It didn't do much for him, though, as he caught two passes for 10 yards over 10 games in what turned out to be his second and final season in the NFL.

The number remained out of circulation until Dez Bryant arrived in 2010.

9 The most famous award in college football and the most famous team in pro football would seem like a perfect match. Only one problem: Guys who win the award tend to be drafted early in the first round, and, for most of their existence, the Cowboys have drafted late. Plus, Dallas went long stretches without needing quarterbacks or running backs, the positions that mostly win the award.

Still, among the hundreds of players in team history, you can find five Heisman winners:

NAME	COLLEGE	YEAR WON HEISMAN	YEAR(S) IN DALLAS
Roger Staubach	Navy	1963	1969-79
Tony Dorsett	Pitt	1976	1977-87
Herschel Walker	Georgia	1982	1986-89, 1996-97
Eddie George	Ohio State	1995	2004
Vinny Testaverde	Miami	1986	2004

Nineteen seventy-seven was the first season the Cowboys had a pair of Heisman Trophy winners, and they won the Super Bowl that season. They got back to the Super Bowl the next year. After falling short in 1979, Staubach retired, leaving Dorsett as the lone Heisman winner, until 1986, when Herschel Walker arrived.

Dorsett didn't like the fact that Walker was making more money than he was and the pairing never really worked. It was an awkward two seasons. But it was somewhat historic; the only previous time a team had two Heisman-winning running backs was in 1984, when the Saints had both George Rogers and Earl Campbell for eight games.

The next time the Cowboys had a Heisman winner, they again had a pair: Testaverde at quarterback and George at running back. Both were well past their prime by the time they played 13 games together in 2004; Dallas went 5-8 in that span.

10 This question also could've been phrased as "name the five players who lasted with the Cowboys across all five Super Bowl appearances in the 1970s."

They were:

- Defensive lineman Larry Cole
- Safety Cliff Harris
- Linebacker D.D. Lewis
- Safety Charlie Waters
- Offensive lineman Rayfield Wright

Can you guess which started all five Super Bowls? Actually, the answer is none. Harris started all but Dallas's first Super Bowl (following the 1970 season), Waters started all but the second (1971), and Cole and Wright all but the fourth (1977). Lewis started three (all but the first two).

Interestingly enough, all five started the middle game (1975).

Note: Roger Staubach started four Super Bowls and was on the roster for the other (1970) but was the only healthy offensive player not sent onto the field.

The other two guys worth highlighting are Charles Haley and Preston Pearson.

Pearson pulled off an amazing trifecta, playing in Super Bowls for the coaching trinity of Don Shula, Chuck Noll, and

Tom Landry. He was with the Colts for the game following the 1968 season (famous for Joe Namath's backing up his guaranteed victory for the Jets), with the Steelers for the Super Bowl following the 1974 season, and with Dallas for the Super Bowls following the 1975, '77, and '78 seasons (two of them against his old pals from Pittsburgh).

As you may recall, Haley won two Super Bowls with San Francisco (1989 and '90), then was with the Cowboys for all three Super Bowls of the Triplets era (1992, '93, and '95).

EXTRA POINT

Congratulations. You've done it. Now you are truly a Dallas Cowboys fan.

To celebrate your blend of passion and knowledge, here's an extra piece of information—an ace in the hole you can use to test anyone who tells you they are a Dallas Cowboys fan.

QUESTION:
Who was the first Dallas Cowboys player ever to touch the ball in a regular season game?

ANSWER:
Tom Franckhauser

A cornerback taken from the Los Angeles Rams with the 16th pick in the expansion draft, Franckhauser started every game of the Cowboys' inaugural season at left cornerback. He was also the primary kick returner.

On Saturday night, September 24, 1960, at the Cotton Bowl, Dallas won the coin toss and elected to receive. Don Sutherin of the Pittsburgh Steelers officially opened the game, the season, and the entire on-field history of the Dallas Cowboys with a kickoff that landed in the arms of Frankhauser. The record shows that he caught it at the 8-yard line and returned it 15 yards.

It's the kind of moment in time that could easily be lost to history. Except to the most diehard Cowboys fans.

ACKNOWLEDGMENTS

As of November 2015, I figured my days of writing books about the Dallas Cowboys were done. Then Julie Ganz of Skyhorse Publishing called. After discussing this new series, I was intrigued by the concept of asking trivia questions and giving answers in the form of a story. It seemed fun to write—and, I hope, it's been fun to read. Special thanks to Julie for letting me take on this challenge and for patiently getting it across the goal line.

Additional thanks go to my wife, Lori, and our sons, Zac, Jake, and Josh for tolerating my slipping into book mode yet again. John McFarland was indispensable in providing advice, insight, and encouragement, and proved to be quite tolerant to all the references of his beloved Vikings' being on the wrong side of Cowboys history.

Shout-outs also go to the folks at Pro-Football-Reference. com for having a website that's an incredible repository of information and for a support team that helped me dig up some details I couldn't find on my own, and to Joe Trahan of the Cowboys PR staff for essentially serving as the holder on the book's extra point.